AMAZON KEYWORDS *for* BOOKS

HOW TO USE KEYWORDS FOR BETTER DISCOVERY ON AMAZON

THE AMAZON SELF PUBLISHER SERIES, BOOK 1

DALE L. ROBERTS

Amazon Keywords for Books: How to Use Keywords for Better Discovery on Amazon

By Dale L. Roberts

Some recommended links in this book are part of affiliate programs. This means if you purchase a product through one of the links, then I get a portion of each sale. It doesn't affect your cost and greatly helps support the cause. If you have any reservations about buying a product through my affiliate link, then feel free to Google a direct link and bypass the affiliate link.

Cover design by a Fiverr seller. To see the full process of how we created the cover design, watch the video at https://dalelinks.com/5designs.

Formatting services provided by Archangel Ink: https://archangelink.com

ISBN: 978-1-950043-14-9

Are you ready to begin your own self-publishing journey?
You have a story.
It deserves to be told.

Learn the fundamentals of self-publishing books...

In this in-depth, yet succinct, course.

The DIY Publishing Course for Beginners

It's perfect for anyone new to the self-publishing business!
It will take you from manuscript to self-published.

The best part? It's 100% free!

Visit DIYPublishing.biz/Free to enroll today.

Keywords ▾ Contents

Preface 1

Introduction 3

Keywords 101 7

Search Engine Algorithms 101 21

Keyword Research 35

Keyword Use on KDP 47

Leveraging Amazon Ads for Better Keywords 57

Building Keyword Relevancy 63

Keyword Tools & Resources 75

Conclusion 80

A Small Ask… 82

About the Author 83

Special Thanks 84

Other Notable Resources 87

References 90

Keywords ▾

Preface

This book is the culmination of over 6 years in the self-publishing business and learning from the best in the industry. Not to mention, I've been running a YouTube channel and building a brand around Self-Publishing with Dale. Inevitably, viewers, followers, and random folks would ask me where they could find my books about self-publishing. I could never recommend any of my books. Why? Because all my books were about fitness and the other books under pen names had nothing to do with self-publishing.

It only makes sense I finally pivot away from fitness publishing and provide insights into the world of self-publishing through, of all things, a self-published book.

I've been struggling for the past couple years to pull the trigger. Between building the Self-Publishing with Dale brand, managing my other self-published assets, and coaching self-publishers, I just never made it a priority.

Well, that all ended when I stopped making excuses and started taking action. There's no better time than now since I've seen a huge influx of new aspiring authors and self-publishers. Rather than hang my hat on simply one publication though, I decided to come out of the gate with a series of three books.

The entire series is based on the most common pain points of authors and self-publishers using the Amazon platform for publishing:

1. Keywords
2. Marketing and promotion
3. Reviews

Sure, you could skip this book and try to piecemeal all the content together from my 450+ videos on YouTube. And, maybe you could find your way through online articles and free courses. The issue is you have to discern what is right or wrong, current or outdated, and relevant or irrelevant. But, what if I could equip you with everything you need to know to take action now? Imagine being able to cut out all the B.S. and get right to the stuff that'll move the needle in your business.

Enter the *Amazon Self Publisher* series.

Amazon Keywords for Books: How to Use Keywords for Better Discovery on Amazon is the best first part in this three-part series. I'm confident once you read through this three-part series, you'll be better equipped to handle the biggest concerns plaguing self-publishers using the Amazon platform.

Enjoy and happy publishing!

–Dale L. Roberts

Keywords

Introduction

Walking into the crowded hotel lobby, I scanned the clusters of people for a familiar face. That situation was already overwhelming, but now imagine my usually introverted mind reeling at the prospect of starting a conversation with a complete stranger. But, that wouldn't have to happen if only I found one person I knew. And, bingo! There he was, Dan Norton. Now, rather than go into the gory details of who Dan is or how we know each other, I'll just say he and I share quite a few mutual loves. One of our shared interests is pro wrestling.

Naturally, as I'm walking up to Dan, I see he's talking to a mutual acquaintance, Andru Edwards. Oddly enough, Andru and I have crossed paths many times, and each time we share a common love – pro wrestling. See where this is going yet? Andru and I are both former pro wrestlers. He'd trained on the east coast, whereas I trained in Calgary, Alberta, Canada. But, it's that bond the two of us share that makes for easy conversation and ways for us to catch up with each other.

At a previous conference where we'd run into each other, I discovered he was trained by one of my all-time favorites. So, when I approached the two, I was elated to discover they were talking about our shared love – pro wrestling. I promise this is going somewhere, just stay with me.

"Hey, Dan, did you know that Andru is a trained pro wrestler?" I asked.

"No, I didn't," Dan responded.

The three of us chatted like excited children. We'd shared favorite matches, favorite wrestlers, locker room etiquette, and the whole shebang. Now and then, folks would wander by us and tune in to our conversation. Another fellow video creator, Mike Vardy, popped into the conversation at one point to share he had a tattoo tribute to his favorite wrestler.

And, though people would briefly visit our small group of wrestling enthusiasts, the four of us stayed. Some people would come to listen in and chime in their favorite parts of the sport. Others would hear a bit about what we were talking about and just move on.

The shared interest and theme of the conversation was pro wrestling. Now, this book isn't so much about pro wrestling at all. In fact, that'll probably be the last you hear of it. It's more about the concept of a conversation or shared interest. That's where keywords lie. I'd imagine had we all not had that shared interest, this would be a bit more stilted and hard to convey. But, we shared this love for pro wrestling, a pre-determined sport that has a niche audience. We would've been limited to the two or three of us had no one had an interest. But, we had a few people who were very much interested or mildly intrigued by what we were talking about.

When people tuned into the conversation, they heard the general theme and the specific word or derivative of "wrestle." That's what kept people coming. And, that's how keywords function in the online ethos. A keyword is a beacon shining from the lighthouse guiding ships away from rocky terrain and onto safer shores. Keywords are the shared interests people have and the way for people to identify with other people. Without keywords, online users would be forced to mindlessly scroll through websites, trying to find what they're looking for.

Sure, every blind squirrel gets a nut. However, without keywords, we'd be lost and forced to figure things out on our own. With keywords, you significantly increase your likelihood of finding precisely what you're looking for.

That's what we did in that crowded lobby that night. The three of us had a shared interest. We spoke about what we loved. We didn't have to think about "profitable" ways to express ourselves, or what was the best way to call a wrestling move. We just talked about it. When people gathered around us, they knew what the conversation was about and if it was of any interest to them.

As you go through this book, you're going to discover more basic concepts that'll help you see an overview of the business of keywords. We'll also dive deeper into more advanced concepts. Even if you were to put this book down now, I'm confident if you follow this advice you'll get pretty far:

> Describe your book in a few words. Don't worry about profitability. Don't worry about trying to gather an audience. Don't worry about saying the right thing or the wrong thing. Just say it. The rest will fall into place.

I know many would-be experts will be quick to correct me. These are the same folks who feel you shouldn't follow your passion. They'd rather have you grind it out and hope for the best. However, I'm going to be real with you. You aren't writing and publishing books for a machine. You're writing and publishing books for people. Real people. Once you get past the whole part of trying to game the system or trick Amazon into doing your bidding, you'll discover that *people* buy books. Algorithms and search engines don't buy books.

But, if you want to increase your odds for success, it's sometimes best to know what to say, how to say it, when you should say it, and where you should say it. That way, you open your circle of influence and welcome more like-minded people. That's what it's about. Grow your circle of friends. Welcome more people into the conversation. And, nurture those relationships. That's when you'll see your audience grow exponentially as the days, weeks, months, and years go on.

I encourage you to read on and take notes as you go. You may have to go back and reread some sections. Lord knows it took me over 6 years to even get this basic understanding of how keywords function on the Amazon marketplace. I don't imagine a short book will get you the same knowledge as I have, but I'll point you in the right direction. By the end of this book, you'll have all the information to select the ideal keywords for publishing your books on Amazon by way of Kindle Direct Publishing. Read on!

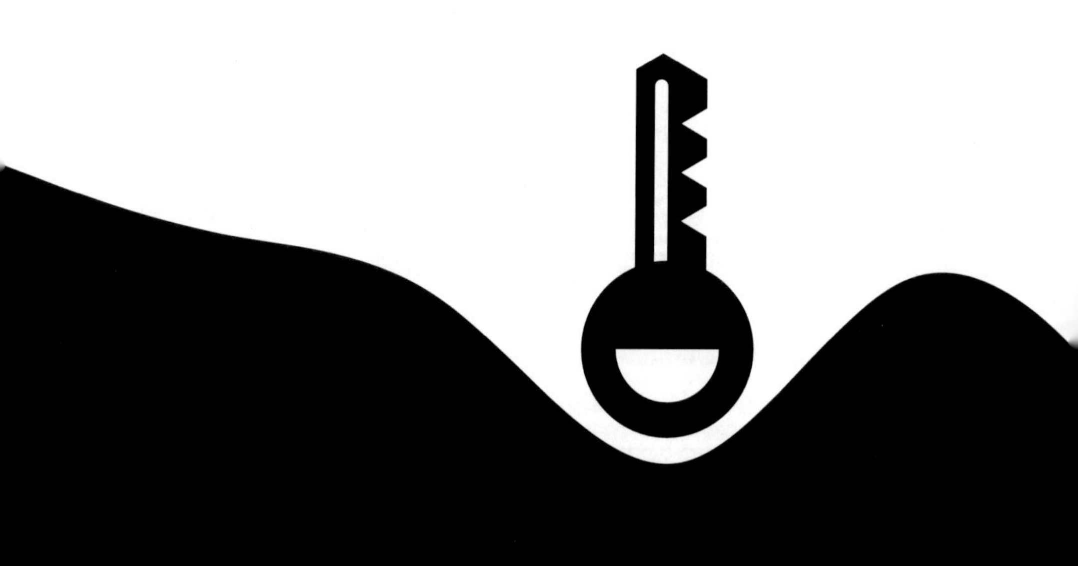

Keywords ▾

Keywords 101

What Are Keywords?

Keywords are the bridge connecting a customer to a potential outcome or product. When you want to learn more about something, you open a browser, type into the search window what you believe you want to find, and the search engine scrapes online options for the best fit. Deeper insights reveal more complexity when it comes to how a search engine finds what it does. For now, just know a keyword is how a customer tries to find something.

Many people misunderstand keywords and view them like a game of *Buzzword* or *Taboo*. The misconception is a keyword only consists of a single word. But, that's the furthest from the truth. In fact, a keyword can be one or more words forming a phrase. Heck, some of the best keywords are phrases that are a string of 3 or more words. Why are they the best? Because it narrows down the search and dramatically increases the odds of a customer finding what they're looking for.

For instance, I might look for ways to exercise. But, I have a litany of injuries and limitations, so not all exercises are going to suit me. If I simply used the keyword "exercise" to search options, I may get a ton of popular exercise options that are unsuitable for me. However, if I target my search a bit more, then my search results will bring back items a bit more appropriate for me. What if I use "back injury exercises" or "exercises to strengthen the back"? Now, I've narrowed down the search to something a lot more appropriate to what I want and need.

We could dive even deeper into our search and get more granular by getting even more specific. Maybe I could search "30-day exercise program to strengthen the back." Wow! Now, I've gotten time-specific in my targeting. And, I've eliminated a whole lot. Can you imagine the results had I just chosen "exercise" as my search query?

If I used "exercise" as my only descriptor to find what I need, I'd be searching for hours to find what would best fit me. But, once I got specific about what I needed, the search engine has more to work with and can narrow down the options.

Try it out for yourself. Go to Amazon and type in the word "exercise." How many results came back? How many of those results interest you or are even suitable for your needs?

Now, get more specific about the type of exercise you want. Get *really* granular in your search. Choose something time-specific, age-based, and goal-based. See what the search results bring back. Most likely, you're going to find more suitable options for your needs.

And, that's how keywords work. They aren't just a single term people use to find what they're looking for. The best keywords are phrases or a string of words that pull up something specific to your wants and needs.

Why Are Keywords Important?

You'd think I hammered the point home with the previous section, but now we have to look at it from a content creator's standpoint. As a writer or publisher, we're always looking for ways to get more sales. Naturally, our minds gravitate towards the best keywords to draw in the most potential customers, but we forget about the human experience in the process. When you try to publish books for an algorithm or search engine, you lose sight of the original point – to sell more books to *people*.

We want to connect with more readers, not search queries. That's why you need to get good on who your audience is.

Identify Your Ideal Reader

Before even putting pen to paper, you should identify your ideal reader. This is the person you want to read your book. No, you should not be writing a book for everyone. Because when you try to please everyone, you'll please no one in the process.

About 6 years ago, when I published my first book, I was quick to share it with anyone and everyone. One of those people was a friend and marketing expert, Mark Stafford. We sat down for a casual lunch when I stuffed my published book into his hands.

The first question Mark asked was, "Who is your target audience?"

"Everyone," I said.

Mark narrowed his vision on the cover, leafed through the book, and appeared to ponder on the best response.

"Everyone? This can't be for everyone. Who do you see buying this book?" he asked.

"Everyone. I made an exercise book good for everyone from kids to senior citizens," I said.

"That's not possible. Senior citizens can't work out the same as kids would. Did you give advice for both in different chapters?"

He stumped me. I really thought my book was meant for everyone. In my mind, it was at the time. But, when I thought about it, I'd never gotten good on who I was writing for. My first book was hammered garbage to put it nicely.

Rather than take Mark's advice to heart, I spent the better part of two years struggling to make ends meet as a full-time author. Why? Because I didn't get good on who my audience was.

Once you identify your ideal reader or your target audience, the rest becomes easier. Much like defining your purpose:

When you identify your why, the how becomes easy.

When I finally identified my ideal reader, I could then begin to figure out why they'd look for my book. Once I figured out my ideal reader's purpose, I then theorized ways they would search for my book. That's what you want to do.

1. Who is your reader?
2. Why are they looking for your book?
3. What is your ideal reader's pain point?
4. How would they look for your book?

Once you answer those four questions, you can then list several keywords as potential candidates. These keywords act as bridges to your products or different avenues leading to your book.

What Are the Different Types of Keywords?

Now comes the nerdy stuff. You don't need to remember the terms and don't worry if you don't get the nuances right away. But, it's a good idea to get a look under the hood, so you know how and why keywords function the way they do. We'll revisit these throughout this book.

The single term keyword phrase is commonly known as the root keyword. In our previous example of "exercise," that was our root keyword. The root signifies the base of the topic. We can all agree exercise takes many forms, so that's why it's the root keyword.

Now, think about other root keywords besides exercise. Here are a few:

- Romance
- Science Fiction
- Politics
- Christianity

Do you see how simple that was? Did you notice what I did in the previous list? There's one keyword that should stick out like a sore thumb. Look back. Do you see it?

"Science Fiction" is the one root keyword with two words in it. How is this a root keyword, then?

Root keywords don't always have to be a single term. They can consist of multiple words. The root keyword is a general category search. As you can imagine, "science fiction" takes many forms, including:

- Science fiction romance
- Military science fiction

- Post-apocalyptic science fiction
- Space opera science fiction
- Werebear shapeshifter romance science fiction

Okay, okay. The last one might be a stretch, but it's more to prove a point that a root keyword is merely a jumping-off point and not so much a single term alone. A root keyword is the most generalized way of identifying a customer's search. It's the other words in the keyword phrase that act as descriptors.

The next type of keyword is a long-tail keyword. As you can imagine, this is a full keyword phrase made up of about three or more words strung together. Long-tail keywords are the most granular approach to searching online. When we built out a search for my exercise needs, we got very specific on time, goals, and special needs. The full phrase represented a long-tail keyword search term.

You won't often hear me say long-tail keyword in the book or on video. Why? Because it's easier for me to say keyword. Could I be more specific? Yes, because then I'd be more precise with my audience. Do you see the mistake I made? I illustrate the importance of using a root keyword versus a long-tail keyword. Rather than using the root keyword of "keyword" alone, I could be more specific. Once I'm more specific, my audience gets a better understanding of what's going on. Pretty cool, right?

That's how long-tail keywords work. When you get specific, your audience gets a better understanding.

Often, I hear would-be experts and self-professed gurus who say self-publishing is saturated. That's furthest from the truth. The fact is many people have tapped into all the root keywords for easy search volume. Now, we're faced with getting more granular with our audience and identifying the many ways customers search for a solution to their problems. The market isn't saturated. Plenty of consumers are still looking for solutions to their problems. You just have to figure out how they're searching.

And, the best part is the consuming audience always changes the way they use search engines. Dialects change, popular trends change, and descriptors change. The market is ever-changing. All you have to do is identify where an opportunity exists and deliver the goods when someone finds your content.

How Can You Search Different Types of Keywords?

Here's where we'll get into the nitty-gritty of keywords because now we'll discuss keyword types. These keyword types are used most commonly in ad campaigns through services like Google Ads, Facebook Ads, and something we'll cover later, Amazon Ads. Knowing the various keyword types will help you refine your approach and possibly leverage the power of online advertising.

Once you get a fundamental understanding of advertising online, you'll be able to pay for data that'll serve you up the exact audience you want. The audience reveals itself through what they're searching to discover your book and if they buy your book based on that search.

If a customer isn't buying, then most likely, there's a disconnect. Now, rather than going into how the book cover and book description play a vital role in the conversion of the sale, we'll simply focus on the keyword that gets them there. What we'll get into later, ultimately, is that the keyword can drive traffic to your book. But, if it doesn't convert into a sale, it may not be the issue with the keyword, especially if it has perceived relevance.

The first type of keyword is a broad match. A broad match keyword is when you have a general search of a keyword that can be configured any way you make it, shake it, or bake it. When using a broad keyword match, you could use a simple keyword like "exercise at home." The search engine is going to play word jumble and selective use with those words.

For instance, a broad keyword match for "exercise at home" could get search volume for:

- Home exercise
- No exercise
- At home recipes
- Home cooking
- Home buying
- Group exercise

Do you see how vague a broad keyword match is? It's like telling the advertising platform to serve up just about anyone. Can you imagine the context of the original conversation about "wrestling?" It would be like if someone came up who was an amateur stand-out and heard us talking about wrestling only to discover it's the sports entertainment variety and not the Olympic-style wrestling.

Broad keyword matches are suitable for advertising campaigns for cheaper clicks. But, with cheaper clicks, you get a larger audience who doesn't want your book. That's okay because you're casting a wide net, identifying the quick victories and low-hanging fruit.

Think of broad keyword matches like this:

Wide net = wide audience + low relevance

The next type of keyword is a broad modifier. These types of keywords are when you're looking for deviations of your broad keyword. Let's go back to our original keyword example, "exercise at home." But, this time in an advertising campaign, we'll use the "+" symbol before a word to identify our need for deviation. You'd place the plus symbol before the word you wish to have a bit more flexibility. This allows for a broader search while getting a bit more granular search results. Rather than limiting it to a specific type of word, we can then use it in many ways.

In this instance, we'd use "+exercise +at +home."

- Exercising at home
- Homesteading
- Homeschooling exercises
- Exercises at the fitness institute
- At the Drive-In

Do you see how the results bring back a crazy list of very different results? But, your chances as an advertiser to identify an audience have significantly increased, especially if you see conversions. And, the best part is it unearths possibilities you'd never thought about. With these new possibilities, you may open yourself to a potential audience you never knew had an interest in your book.

Think of broad modified keywords like this:

Wide net with flexibility = wide audience + more granular

Try this fun little test out. Go to Google and type in "+exercise +at +home" and see what results you get. I'm sure it'll be way different than my random examples above. Take note of all the possibilities and pay the closest attention to the bolded words in each search result. That represents the broad modified match.

The broad modified keyword presents more flexible search results like this example.

The next two keyword types are the holy grails of keywords. Once you get these keywords dialed in, you'll most likely have killer ad campaigns and a book with crazy organic traffic. This means you'll be getting a high return on investment for your ads, and people will find your book easily with the keywords you've selected.

The first of the two holy grail keyword types is exact match. An exact match is when a customer uses a keyword, and your book gets served based on exactly matching your keyword. Ultimately, if you're running any ad campaigns, you'll want to leverage the power of broad and broad modified keywords. Then, identify exact keywords that lead to the sale of your book. Those exact keywords are the exact matches you'll use in future ad campaigns because they were successful in turning a browsing customer into a buyer.

It's the exact match keyword that will often be the best selection for your book's information. Will you be able to rely on an exact match forever? Most likely not, but you'll soon discover the power of relevancy and the shelf-life of a keyword.

Often, an exact match is represented by quotes around the keyword. Try this out for yourself. Go to Google and search for "exercises at home" but include the quotes this time. What you're doing is telling the search engine you want only *exercises at home* and no deviation of that.

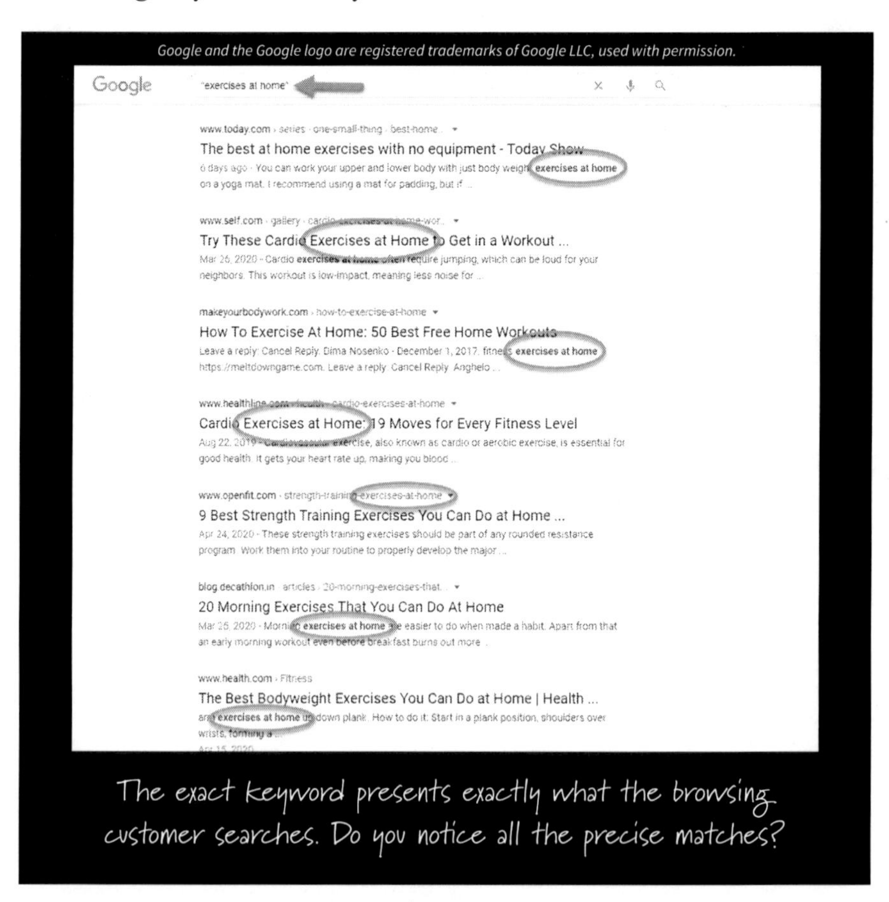

Google and the Google logo are registered trademarks of Google LLC, used with permission.

The exact keyword presents exactly what the browsing customer searches. Do you notice all the precise matches?

The help page for Kindle Direct Publishing even discourages publishers from using quotes in their seven keyword slots (covered later in the book). Why? Because it dramatically inhibits the number of searches since you're not allowing for any wiggle room. I'll agree wholeheartedly on that point. You can use exact matches in an ad campaign, and in most instances, you won't have to use the quotes. However, avoid using the quotes in your book's information, because you diminish the ability to reach more readers and search queries.

As you build out and scale up your ad campaigns, you ultimately want to have exact match keyword campaigns. But you also want to build up an ad campaign with the next keyword variation, the phrase match.

The phrase match works along with exact matches the same way a broad modified keyword works with broad keywords, but a keyword phrase match is asking for the exact keyword with some variation or deviation. This way, it opens your campaign's or book's likelihood of discovery to more audiences. It will also reveal other possibilities that'll work in your favor.

When it comes to exact match and phrase match, remember this:

Exact Match = Smallest net = exact audience + higher relevance + hyper-targeted audience

Phrase match = Exact keyword with variation = smaller net + higher relevance + targeted audience

As you read on, you might find this section a bit muddy since it's merely laying the groundwork. Get at least a basic understanding of these concepts. Then, you can better grasp the more advanced concepts as we move along. Do you need to run ad campaigns to be successful? No, but do you increase your odds of success using paid advertising? Possibly. As long as you know what you're doing. At the end of the book, you'll get some of my trusted resources and reliable experts in advertising.

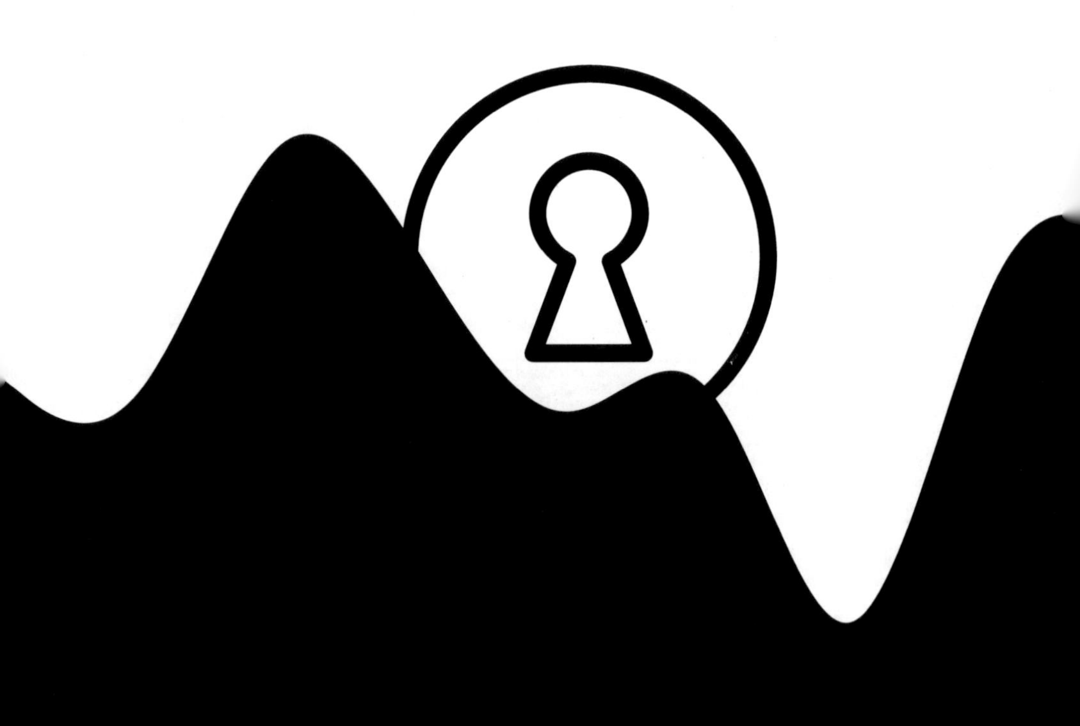

Keywords ▾ **Search Engine Algorithms 101**

How Does a Search Engine Work?

Oddly enough, a lot of how keywords work is through the power of the search engine. But, the search engine is simply what the audience sees as a website with a box where you type up something you want to find online. Even so, it's far more complicated than you'd think. No, there's no magical gnomes who read your mind and serve you the precise thing you want. And, no, it's not as simple as the search engine guessing what a browsing consumer wants.

Search engines function on algorithms, a complex mathematical formula. After years of billions of search queries, Google has algorithmic programming down to a science. And, the Google algorithm becomes more complex and sophisticated with every passing day and every single search.

In layman's terms, an algorithm is a formula that tries to predict user behavior based on past user behaviors and related behaviors of similar audiences. For instance, when a browsing customer searches for "home-cooked recipes for weight loss," the search engine gets to work in a few ways. It figures out what's the best fit for the customer based on previous search history, past consuming habits, and other people who share the same types of behaviors. Crazy, right?

A search engine serves results to a browsing consumer based on relevance. For the sake of less confusion, I'm going to separate two types of relevance. When I refer to relevance by itself, then I mean algorithmic relevance. The second type is perceived relevance or what we believe to be relevant to a book or search query.

Algorithmic relevance is based on a formula and a potentially positive outcome. When a consumer searches for something and they don't find it, then the algorithm will determine the results weren't relevant to the consumer. However, when a consumer searches and clicks to view more content or even buys an item, the algorithm adjusts. It will then deem the search result with a positive outcome as relevant to the search term.

On Amazon, if a customer searches for "nursery rhymes for babies," the algorithm is going to view past behaviors based on this search term. It's going to review the products with the best results and conversions – be it sales or views – and serve the customer several product suggestions. But wait, it gets a little more complicated. The Amazon algorithm is going to account for previous search history, buying behavior, and other similar customer search history and buying behaviors. Then, the Amazon algorithm serves up the products it theorizes to be the most relevant to that customer.

This is what a lot of would-be experts in self-publishing get wrong time and again. They elude to finding the magical keyword or keyword phrase methodology. And, they'll even share some best practices for finding a keyword the purest way possible. But, what they fail to realize is the algorithm isn't a one-size-fits-all formula. It's more customized to each browsing customer's needs. Based on what that customer does next, the algorithm adjusts accordingly.

If you ever want to test it out, I recommend you search for any random item on Amazon. Choose something you'd never buy. Click on the product, read the full description, and then scroll down and choose additional products related to it. Spend about 20 to 30 minutes doing this. In fact, add a few of the items to your shopping cart (don't worry, you don't have to buy them).

Now, take a break from Amazon for a day or two. Then, come back to Amazon on its home page and discover all the items it'll serve you. It'll be a weird mixture of what you usually like and then this random item you'd never buy.

It's kind of like going onto a used car lot and telling the salesman you're interested in a Mercedes Benz, and you want to see all the models. The used car salesman might be confused because he clearly saw you rolling into the parking lot in your beat-up 1997 Ford Ranger. But, he's gonna go with it. Then, after you're done shopping, you leave and come back and tell him you're interested in buying a truck. That used car salesman is going to be so confused because he thought you wanted something a bit more luxury-related. But, he's still not surprised you want to look at trucks since that's what you originally arrived in.

The Amazon algorithm is a fickle beast, and anyone who tells you they know precisely how it acts is a little full of themselves or something else altogether. The Amazon algorithm bases its actions on consumer actions and reactions, then adjusts from there.

And, that's where reality versus perception comes into play. Where we think we know the answer, the algorithm has more in-depth insights than we can even begin to fathom. So, while we can theorize a keyword set will bring success to a book, the algorithm will ultimately decide if the customers genuinely want it. And, if you're a new author who has published your first book, you're working on rolling a boulder uphill.

The fewer books you have as an author, the fewer opportunities you have to gain the favor of the Amazon algorithm.

Are Search Engine Algorithms the Same Across Platforms?

Are search engine algorithms the same across all platforms? Is the Google search engine algorithm the same as the Amazon algorithm? Or, is the Facebook algorithm the same as the Amazon algorithm? Though the principles are somewhat the same, the audience is different. After all, the audience might be different ages and from different regions. The audience might have different languages or different dialects. Each audience has a different belief system and different needs. And, the most critical part is the actual audience size per platform and the amount of time the search engine has been used.

Google, by far, is the most sophisticated of all search engines. Why is that? It's because it is the most popular and most widely used search engine in the world. The more customers use Google, the more the algorithm begins to refine its search results. And, the more repeat customers Google has, the more the algorithm can predictively serve results that most match a customer's wants and needs.

Google has been getting billions of searches since its inception, so it has a leg up on all search engines across every platform. So, where does that leave Amazon? A few years ago, I read an article stating that Amazon's search engine is about 5 years behind Google's. The reason? Though Amazon is the online retail juggernaut, its online traffic pales in comparison to what Google has.

That doesn't mean Amazon's algorithm is archaic by any stretch. It's still rather sophisticated, but think of Amazon's algorithm like the little brother to the Google algorithm. Since Google dominates search traffic, it behooves every business using a search engine algorithm to take notes and implement what they're doing. That equates to more repeat customers and, most importantly, happy customers. After all, if you can get more people what they want out of life, then you can get everything you want too. That's how search engines function – to deliver the best results possible to the consumer.

As the world shifted in early 2020 to social distancing, now more than ever, online sales and traffic are a necessity. That means more consumer traffic will help to refine search engine algorithms. Amazon will start to pick up steam since customers who used to be steadfast about ordering products in a store are now forced to buy from the online retailer.

If you look at social media platforms, you'll discover quite a few functions on a search engine. Facebook, for example, has a search engine algorithm. And, quite a bit of it is about discovering what their users want most so they can deliver the goods. Then, Facebook leverages that information for online advertising dollars. Is Facebook's algorithm as sophisticated as Google or Amazon? Not by any stretch. But again, it has the same fundamental principles as both those search engine algorithms do.

Even if you were to quit reading this book right now, I'd implore if you want to master the art of keywords, then study search engine algorithms. Then apply what you know about your ideal audience, and you've got a winning formula. How do you begin to understand relevance? Also, how do you build algorithmic relevance for your book?

How Do You Build Relevance for a Keyword?

How exactly do you get a book to be relevant for a given keyword? In theory, if you find a keyword with high search volume and low competition or use, then you should be able to win, right? Not really. I've tested that theory dozens of times. And, though a few might catch lightning in a bottle, the vast majority of authors and publishers don't. Why is that? It has a lot to do with getting your chance to shine and dropping the ball.

For the record, Amazon loves new products. In fact, they love new products so much, Amazon even created a special category for new publications called New Releases. This works for both fiction and nonfiction and in print books and ebooks. The first thirty days of publishing a book are magical on Amazon. Once you publish your book, the clock starts ticking. If you cannot prove to be a winning commodity, you'll be buried in the search traffic after the first month.

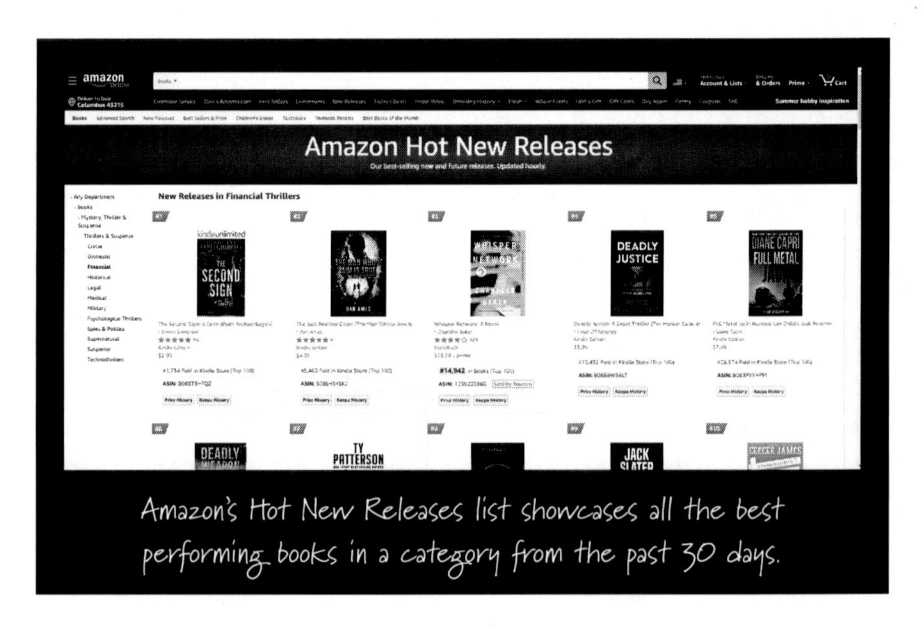

Amazon's Hot New Releases list showcases all the best performing books in a category from the past 30 days.

At the end of the day, the place every author covets is the first-page search results. Why? Because let's face it, not many consumers make it past the first page. Some will hardly scroll down the page to see the full results. Creator of Publisher Rocket and Kindlepreneur.com, Dave Chesson, said the highest converting spot to be was in the first position of the first-page search results. After that, your odds of converting a sale diminish the further down your book is in search results. Then, oddly enough, your odds increase at the last spot of the first-page search.[1]

Is it as simple as adding a keyword to your book's information? Can you simply identify a profitable keyword, put it in your book info, and get the first-page placement? Not really. Remember, the search engine algorithm customizes search results to each customer based on their browsing history and buying patterns.

So, what builds algorithmic relevance? Quite a few items help in building relevance for your title. Of course, the king of all metrics is the sale. If you can get a sale, then you've got a chance. But, that doesn't explain how some titles start winning right after publishing with no advertising and no real audience. Enter impressions.

As mentioned before, Amazon loves new products and wants to give any new product a shot. So, it'll start to serve a book to an audience based on the keywords used and the categories selected for a book. When a customer searches for a book on Amazon and Amazon serves the results, that's when an impression occurs. Once Amazon presents a product to a customer, it's known as an impression.

> Fun fact: In Amazon Advertising, impressions are free. This is a further reason to use Amazon Advertising to build relevance for your book.

The next most crucial action comes when the customer makes a decision. Does the customer continue to scroll and look at the next page of results? If so, then the recommended products proved to have less relevance to that customer. That doesn't mean Amazon won't serve those results again. But, it does mean that based on the customer's browsing behavior and buy patterns, Amazon is less likely to serve those products again.

So, in some instances, an unheard-of book gets it's one time to shine through a search query. If a browsing customer passes the chance to view more about the product, then the algorithm has less confidence in this product's ability to fulfill the customer's needs.

Whereas, if a book comes up in a search query and the customer clicks on the book display to see its product page, the customer sends a signal to Amazon. This signal builds relevance for the book. The increased relevance brings more ability to be served to other customers with similar browsing behaviors and buying patterns. Is this starting to make sense? No? Well, let's keep it going.

Sadly, a few years ago, Amazon became the stomping grounds for bad actors who figured out the ability to build relevance on a product through clicks. So, what did they do? They hired people to search for their product and click the product display to view the product page. Also known as click farms, these groups of bad actors would manipulate the algorithm to favor their products simply through clicks alone.

Thankfully, Amazon was fully aware of this hack and immediately tweaked the algorithm to identify false clicks. In turn, sellers of the products getting the absurd amount of clicks with no sales were banned, and their products were removed. So, before you start thinking the name of the game is to search for your book and click on the product page, don't do it. Amazon will detect false clicks and suppress your book listing and, in due time, remove you from the platform. Then, you will have wasted your time and money on a book about leveraging the power of keywords on Amazon for your books.

Also, it's important to note how Amazon will serve your book up with other relevant publications and their product pages. We'll discuss that in more advanced chapters. Those times are also considered impressions. If someone clicks on the product to view the page, then that click counts toward relevancy. Even if your book isn't showing up when searching, your book might be served through other means, including additional product pages and even Amazon's home page. And, Amazon can share your book through its email newsletter for customers.

So, we know impressions are when customers see your book through a search query, product page, or email. Clicks are when a customer visits your book's product page. The next step in the process and the most critical in building relevance is the sale. Is the browsing customer buying your book when they visit your product page? If not, then you've got a problem.

The most common issue when it comes to not getting a click is a bad book cover. When it comes to sales, if a customer is not buying, then chances are likely your book description isn't on-point. You have to compel the browsing customer into buying your book. But, let's pretend for a minute your book cover and description are on-point. And, let's remove the possibility of window shoppers or people lacking the funds to buy your book.

Why wouldn't a person buy your book? You have a great book cover. Otherwise, they wouldn't be compelled to see more about your book when they clicked on your product. Let's say your book description is on-point. So, why didn't they buy it? Most likely, the keywords you're using are a mismatch with the audience. But, I only adjust the keywords once I've changed the previous elements first. Because if you get sales, then you'll build relevancy for the keywords you have. Unless your keyword choice is so off the wall that they make no sense for your book, then your chances of building relevancy greatly diminishes.

A few other metrics help in determining relevancy for your title. Rather than go exhaustively into each item, I'll focus on a few that make the most difference. These last items revolve around product page engagement. Whatever drives the browsing customer to take action on your page beyond sales is typically a good thing. Unless they click "report abuse." In that instance, you've got a troll on your hands, or you've done something severely wrong.

Engagement comes in a variety of forms, but the biggest and most effective of all is the review. Yep, you should've seen this one coming! When a customer leaves a review on your product page, it builds relevancy for your product. When a conversation happens through comments, it aids in more relevancy. The more consistently the reviews and comments occur on a product page, the more relevant the product becomes.

This is just one example of how author Michael Matthews responds to reviews.

However, I don't encourage you to make review gathering the central part of your business. But, you should make it at least a small piece of your business because the book review works in your favor in two ways:

1. Social proof – third-party credibility goes a long way. Regardless if it's good or bad, a review is proof somebody else experienced your product and took the time to share the experience.

2. Relevance – this small social trigger sends a signal to the algorithm notifying Amazon that people are talking about this product.

However, pay the closest attention to this advice here. Never, under any circumstances, get fake reviews to bolster relevancy for your title. As Amazon identifies bad actors and their dastardly ways, they build automated systems to identify false or biased reviews.

While we're discussing what you shouldn't do with your reviews, avoid getting reviews from people who are not your ideal reader. In the past, I thought you should have your friends and family buy and review your book. I don't subscribe to that belief anymore. Why? Because it messes up the algorithm and begins serving your book through impressions to the wrong audience.

Remember when I had you search for a random product you'd never buy? Then, you got served other similar products despite having no interest? Well, that's what holds true here. If you have your mom leave a review despite her being only a fan of quilting and cat books, then the algorithm is going to think your book should be served to audiences like your mom. This can be a disaster for you, especially if you're publishing werebear shapeshifter books. Your mother's local needle worker's guild might be appalled by the suggestion and immediately click away from your product or ignore it altogether.

Then, your book's one time at bat is a fail; therefore, it drops in relevancy.

As an author who gets reviews, you can decide whether to respond to all reviews or no reviews at all. Yes, that means if you're going to bask in the showering praise of the 5-star reviews, then you need to humble yourself in the mud puddles of 1-star snarky reviews. Treat all reviews professionally and never under any circumstance, get defensive. If you need to get defensive, then don't comment.

Why do you want to comment on a review? Ahem, have you been taking notes or keeping up with me? If so, your guess would've been

– relevancy! Yes, commenting on a review builds relevancy and is 100% acceptable and safe. Again, if you're going to comment on one, you should comment on them all. Just be prepared to take it on the chin. All good authors get low reviews. It's not a matter of "if," it's a matter of "when." Just respond tactfully.

The next action that'll lead to more relevancy for your title is the social share. You'll notice on every product page the ability to share to platforms like Facebook, Twitter, Pinterest, and email. Using those options is a great way to share your product and bring in more customers. You also build relevance for your given set of keywords, especially if a customer brought your book up in a search query. Pretty cool, huh?

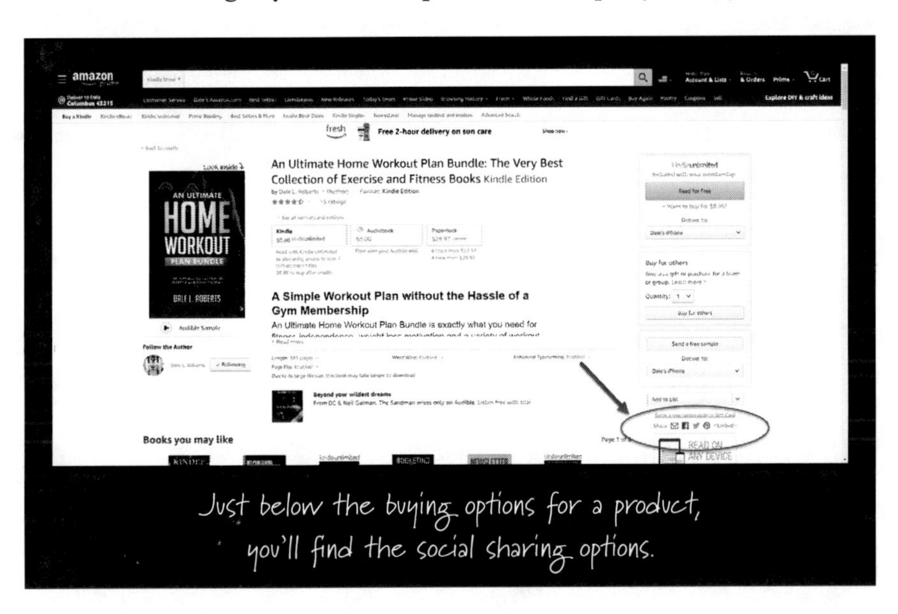

Just below the buying options for a product, you'll find the social sharing options.

Lastly is the ability to add a product to a list. Customers can build wish lists on Amazon where they can store items they would like to buy later on. And, this especially becomes great around the holidays because special categories exist for the sake of gift-giving. So, if you have a social following or an email list, recommend that they add your book to their wish list if they can't afford it now.

Amazon Customers can build wish lists by selecting the "Add to List" dropdown just below the buying options for a product.

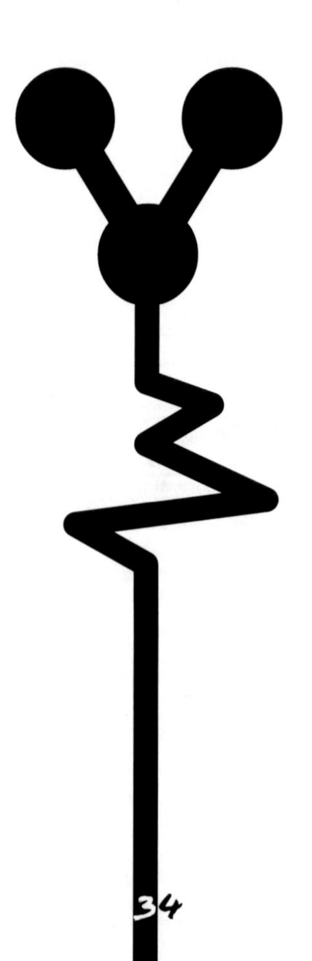

Keywords ▾ **Keyword Research**

How Do You Research Keywords?

Now that you have the basis of how keywords function, how exactly do you find the right keywords? And, what do you need for implementing them in the right way? After all, you don't just want to have any old keywords. You also want to have the right keywords that'll bring you more of a buying audience who'll snatch up a copy of your latest book.

The first and most important rule when it comes to keyword research is to never do your research on a naked browser. Yes, I said that with the intention of you thinking what you're thinking. This means you should never do keyword research through your regular browser alone. Assuming you've been on Amazon before, the algorithm is going to tailor search results based on your previous search history and buying patterns. Your results will be significantly skewed, so you should start with a clean slate.

Can we log out of Amazon and hope for the best? Sure, but even then, they'll track your search history as you research.

The best way to start with a clean slate and keep it clean is to use incognito mode. If you're using a Chrome browser, simultaneously press CTRL, Shift, and the letter N when you have the normal browser open. A black browser should appear with a spy logo on the page. If you're using a different browser type, simply Google a way to get incognito mode on your browser.

Head over to Amazon. For ease of research, I highly recommend you bookmark Amazon.com, the Amazon Kindle Store, and the Amazon Book Store. Since you'll be coming to each spot frequently, it's a good idea you save yourself the time of typing it out in your browser every time. When doing keyword research, be sure to research based on the product type. So, the keywords you use on your Kindle ebook should be a slightly different set of keywords than your print books. Why? Relevancy!

Each product brings a different customer type and different tastes. Therefore, the way a print book customer searches content will be slightly different than of a Kindle ebook customer. That's not to say there's no keyword overlap. Some keywords are the same across both publications but don't solely rely on using the same keywords for both products.

Before you attack the Amazon marketplace, I recommend going in with a checklist and a slight game plan. Spend about thirty minutes jotting out various descriptors for your book's content. Nothing is off the table. The more you can describe, the better. If your book is fiction, write out common tropes in your niche, character types, story arcs, settings, and the like.

If your book is nonfiction, write down common problems, solutions, and run the gamut of phrases related to your niche. Remember, folks, nothing is off the table. Now is not the time to allow your inner editor. Don't worry about proper punctuation or how to spell correctly. You just want a checklist of sorts to help guide you through your session.

Let's focus on researching keywords for ebooks. Keep in mind, the steps are the same for print books. Just make sure to use the same list twice, but keep the results separate. If you unearth common keywords in your ebook keyword research, write them down on your checklist for when you do print book research. Now, open your browser in incognito mode and go to the Kindle ebook store. Type in your word, term, or phrase. I recommend starting with just one word. Then, pause.

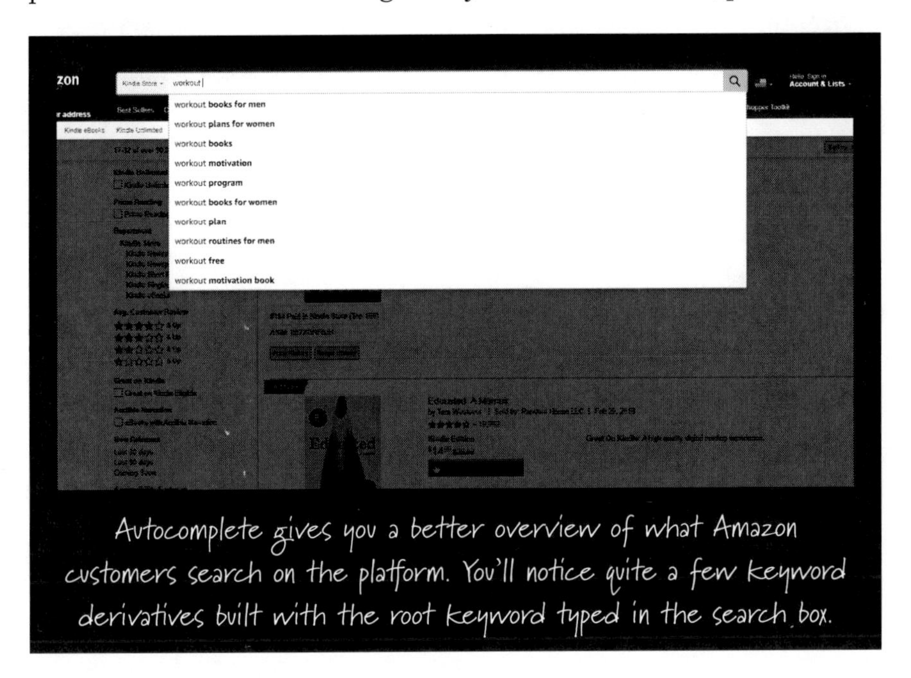

Autocomplete gives you a better overview of what Amazon customers search on the platform. You'll notice quite a few keyword derivatives built with the root keyword typed in the search box.

The Amazon algorithm is going to get to work and give you common suggestions. A dropdown menu will pop up, showing several keyword phrases with the term you're using as a root keyword. You can do one of two things:

1. Take a screenshot – then use these pictures later for the keyword phrases
2. Jot down the perceived relevant keyword phrases – granted, you're not the algorithm whisperer, so you're going to have to go with your gut. But, you'll know if a term isn't relevant based

> on if someone asked you about it in a question. Let's say you have a fitness book for men over forty, and you see fitness books for women over sixty. Chances are likely, you won't perceive any relevance with that keyword and your title.

With your browser in incognito mode, the algorithm doesn't know what to serve you. So, it's going to give you broad and generalized suggestions that are most popular. Not all keywords are going to work. In some instances, you might type out a root keyword or keyword phrase that goes absolutely nowhere. A general rule is if the autosuggest dropdown menu populates with at least one keyword, then it's a usable keyword phrase. If not, cross it off your list.

As you go through your original list, you should have a list of more refined keywords. Heck, the list might outgrow your original one. That's okay because the next process is when we're going to separate the studs from the duds. For now, don't worry about guessing if they're proven or not. We just need a list of possibilities. Once you get into the swing of the next few steps, you'll eliminate quite a few of them based on what we find later.

If you start to hit a dead end and need more ideas, use the keyword alphabet concept. Simply type in your root keyword, then hit the space bar. Now, type the letter "A." Wait for the autosuggest. Jot down any relevant keywords. Then, hit the backspace and try "B." Cycle through the whole alphabet to get a long list of keywords. Don't worry, we'll separate out what works best for your title.

Now that you've got a fully curated list, you're going to take all perceived relevant keywords and finally finish the search. So, type in the full keyword and hit Enter. We want to see what Amazon brings back. But, we're not going to settle for just any old keyword.

How many products are pulled up in the search? You'll see this number in the top left corner of the Amazon page. Amazon shows the first sixteen products out of several products. If you see there's sixteen or less products, we might be dealing with a dud. In that case, you can throw out the keyword.

After completing a search, you'll see how many products appear for a given keyword in the top left corner below the search window.

However, if you find a keyword with thousands of products, then you're dealing with a ton of competition. That's not a bad thing! Competition breeds innovation. If you want to be heard above the noise and use a keyword in a competitive market, then you need to lead with your A-game. But, we'll sort out whether it's worth it or not in the next steps.

Generally, I like to see the number of products below 1,000. If you get up to 10,000 products and you're not an established author, you're going to find it hard to place in the first-page search results. It's especially more difficult after launching with no sales and no advertising. When you start getting higher than 10,000 products, cross the keyword off your list. Or, think about expanding on that keyword. Have autosuggest help you.

Let's say the search results for "home workout plan" have 20,000 products in search. Then, we'd go back to the search bar, type in "home workout plan," space, and then use the keyword alphabet method. You should uncover other options that'll get you a more granular, long-tail keyword with fewer search results.

The old adage holds true in that you want to be a big fish in a small pond. As your sales grow, you can expand into other shorter, broader keyword phrases with more products. For now, conquer the small pond until your book gets off the ground and selling regularly.

Now, focus on the first sixteen products served. These are what the Amazon algorithm deems to be most relevant at that moment in time. It should be noted, relevancy is never constant. It's much like an ocean in that waves will come and go. There will be an ebb and flow to all searches. So, you might search for one keyword in one minute and get a particular search volume. But, in the next, you'll get an altogether different set of products. That's how fickle and somewhat unpredictable the algorithm is.

Scroll down the products page. Skip all the ads. You'll know the ads if you see the word "Sponsored" at the top. Focus on the first sixteen products that aren't an ad. Take note on a few things including:

1. Keyword use – focus on the title, subtitle, series name, description, author bio, the editorial section.
2. Reviews – how many reviews does that book have. The more reviews, the tougher it'll be to compete for first-page placement against that book.

3. Publication date – some information is only accessible on the product page. In that case, click on the product and scroll down to the product details.

4. Amazon Bestseller Rank (ABSR) – This is huge, and in no way should you skip past it. The closer the ABSR is to #1, the more the book sells. The further away from #1, the less the book sells.

Towards the end of this book, I'm going to recommend some resources for shortening your research time. However, instead of sounding like some shill trying to push you on products, I'm teaching you the hard and long way of doing things. So, click on the book's product page and browse the product page. Scroll to the middle of the page to view the product details. You'll see the publication date, the ABSR, the customer reviews, and the imprint.

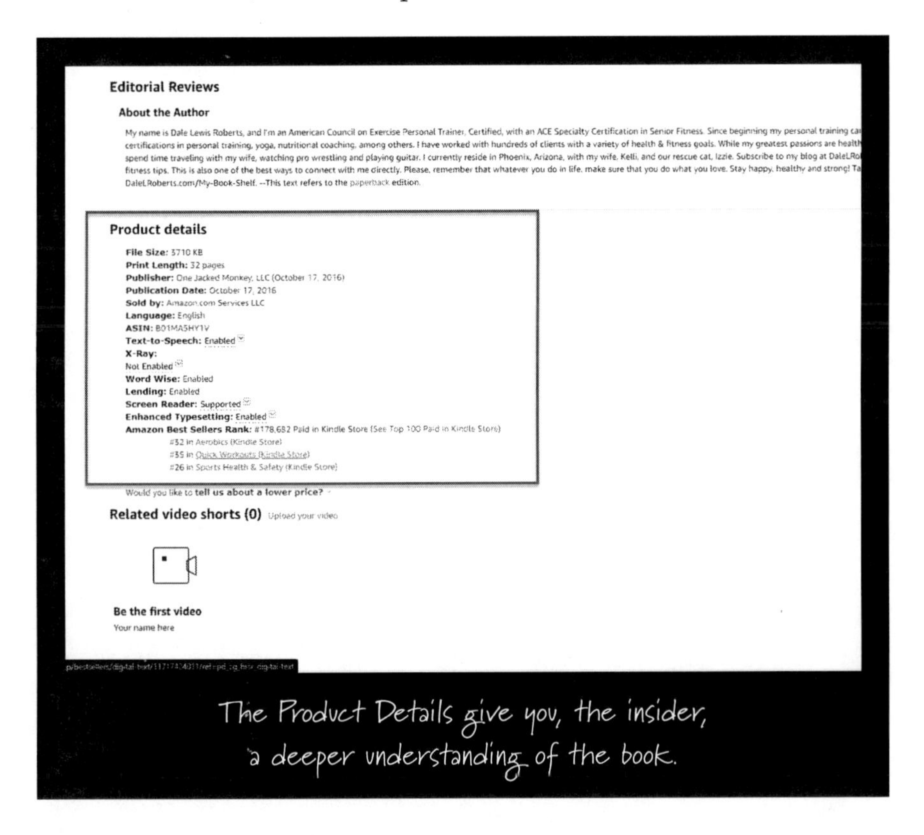

The Product Details give you, the insider, a deeper understanding of the book.

> Fun Fact: If the book's imprint lists "Independently Published," then chances are likely this is a book published through Kindle Direct Publishing.

Keyword Use

If a book has a keyword in the title or subtitle, this publication has nearly cemented the possibility of being pulled up in the search for that term. It doesn't assure it, but it certainly increases the odds. Next, if the book has the keyword in the description, author bio, and editorial section, these are other small triggers building relevancy for this title. Keep in mind, we're not looking for someone who is shoe-horning keywords into every nook and cranny. We're more mindful of what they're doing.

Reviews

As mentioned before, reviews are the lifeblood of social proof and aid in building relevancy. Whether acting as an algorithmic trigger or as a social trigger, reviews play an integral part in proof of concept. If there are a ton of reviews and you plan to share the same shelf space as a book, then plan on catching up somewhat to or competing against this book.

Publication Date

Based mostly on the ABSR, an older publication with a good rank might be proof this book isn't moving anywhere. And, something with staying power is something to model. Do not plagiarize or copy what they're doing. Take notes on common keywords, cover concepts, number of reviews, and more. A book with staying power and decent rank has subtle clues on what you need to do to elevate your book sales.

Amazon Bestseller Rank (ABSR)

This is huge! Generally, I like to see an ABSR under 100,000. To hit #100,000 on the Amazon marketplace, you need at least one sale every day. That's it! Crazy right? With one purchase per day, almost anyone can do it, especially with the right marketing and promotion plan. However, I don't want to see the rank drop below #10,000. Would it be bad if it was closer to #1? No, but again, you're putting yourself into a very competitive niche.

A book with #10,000 ABSR sells about 15 copies per day. That's undoubtedly achievable for most anyone! If you're new, don't fret, you'll get there with persistence and consistency.

> To see an estimate of how many book sales per day it takes to hit a specific ABSR, visit DaleLinks.com/Calculator.

On the first-page search results, I want to see an average ABSR between #10,000 and #100,000. This shows proof of concept. Meanwhile, it also proves with even a soft launch, I should build some relevance on my chosen keywords. I can further cement the relevance for those keywords with an Amazon ad campaign.

Don't feel discouraged if you're finding keywords that are too competitive or not competitive at all. Part of keyword research is going to require intuition. You'll have to go with your gut when choosing. Will you make the best choices as a newbie? Probably not. Trust me, I've gone back to publications I launched in 2014 and cringe at the keyword selection.

The only way to build your intuition is through time and practice. Stick with it, and in due time, you'll find your gut will guide you in the right direction.

Remember the algorithm is ever-changing. Select the keywords you believe best fit your publication at that moment. In due time, you'll want to adjust your keywords if your sales figures aren't quite what you want. However, if your book sales are up and consistent, don't touch your keyword choices. You obviously did something right, so if it isn't broken, don't fix it.

Keep in mind, some keywords are trending and hot in one moment, and no longer of any importance in the next. It had its fifteen minutes of fame, and it's done. I know everyone, and their mother was all over "Apple Cider Vinegar," "Coconut Oil," and "Paleo Diet" in 2014. Now, those topics are hardly pulling in much revenue these days. They've been replaced by "Mindfulness," "Instapot Recipes," and "Keto Diet." Eventually, those will phase out.

Some keywords are evergreen. Rest assured, if it's evergreen, a traditionally published book (trad pub) will typically be at the top of the search. Why? Because they have major advertising, a larger following, and broader reach. So, if you dig around and find a keyword with quite a few trad pub books in the first-page search, then you may want to consider other keyword options.

Not to be confused, you should still check on keywords at least once per year to see if it fits your publication. If your book isn't selling many copies, then you can consider switching out keywords every ninety days. Relevance is variable and ever-changing, but not so much that you want to replace your keyword selections every other day.

When choosing keywords, you're forced to make decisions loosely based on what you see externally. It's hard to tell what a book has done to be successful or get first-page placement. And, even though you may not find your book on first-page placement through incognito mode, it doesn't mean it's not getting served to customers.

Amazon has millions of visitors at any one given moment. They need your product and will serve it to people who seem the best fit. If that doesn't convert a sale, then chances are likely, you'll need to change your approach.

Just don't sweat it too much if you don't see your book pulled up on first-page searches. Somewhere else in some other part of the world, a customer just might be getting your book on a first-page search. The Amazon algorithm customizes the search results based on the customer, not you!

Lastly, before you throw this book across the room and give up on this whole thing, just know it takes time. You aren't going to master this entire thing overnight. And, it will take time and dedication to get your book relevant in the algorithm. In the meantime, do your research and take your time carving out the best choices for your book.

Never guess what keywords go into the seven keyword spots. You're leaving your business to chance, and merely putting in any old keyword off the top of your head will have marginal, if any, results. Friends don't let friends guess their keyword selections.

Once you've got your list whittled down to about 12-24 good keywords, it's time to get to work. As you're researching your keywords, I recommend highlighting any keywords you see as winners. You'll know when it seems right.

As a hypothetical example, I search "YA Science Fiction Romance":

- 250 products
- Average ABSR of 50,000
- Mostly independently published books
- Very few reviews on all books

I'd be all over that and highlight that as a usable keyword.

However, if the same example pulled up this:

- 20,000 products
- Average ABSR 1,000,000
- One trad pub book and the rest are independently published
- Scores of reviews

Then, I'd cross the keyword off the list. There aren't many sales, and assuming the trad pub book is pulling in the vast majority of the sales, then this keyword has low proof of concept. Some keywords might look worth it but prove quickly to be complete flops.

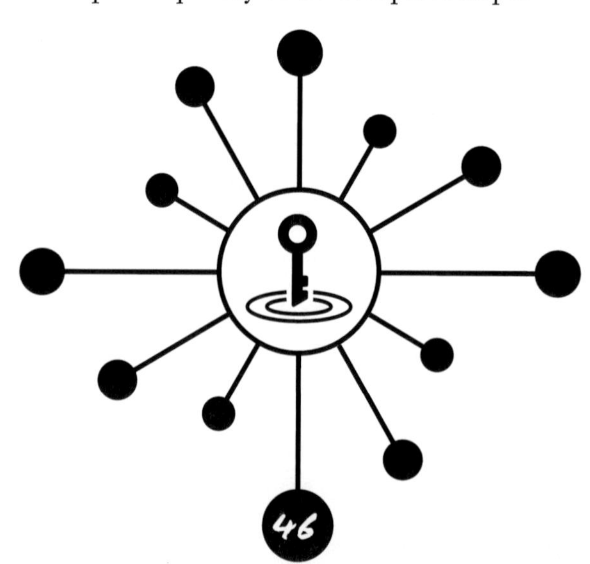

Keyword Use on KDP

Now that you have a long list of keywords, what do you do with them? If you've already written and published the work, a couple of recommendations won't work out for you. But, the rest are universally applicable. Whatever you do, don't delist and republish a book simply to take advantage of all these tips. Simply adjust what you have and push forward!

Where do you use your list of keywords? We're going to focus on the book's metadata or the information that represents the book that includes:

- Title
- Subtitle
- Series Name
- Description
- Seven Keyword Slots

The prime real estate is going to be in the title and subtitle. But, don't force a keyword into a title if it doesn't make sense. For instance, most fiction book titles won't work having a keyword in them. At one point, people were doing that to gain the favor of the algorithm. Those days are coming to an end. The Amazon customer is becoming more discerning. While the customer wants to read werebear shapeshifter romance books, they don't specifically want a book called Werebear Shapeshifter Romance Book. It's weird, comes off clunky, and reeks of amateur hour.

For nonfiction authors, you have free reign on how you do it. But, be tasteful. Go back to any of my old publications and see how I squeezed as many keywords into the title and subtitle as I could. It worked back then, but now, not so much. Pick the keyword that best identifies your book and slip it into your title or subtitle.

It's believed how using keywords in your title and subtitle greatly increases your chances of first-page placement in searches, but, it's not promised to you. Especially if your book has proven less relevant than other choices. The other thing to be mindful of is other books using the same exact title.

Do not under any circumstances use another book title that's on the market. Don't try to build a deviation or derivative of another title. You're a creative entrepreneur, so the worst thing you can do is stifle your creativity and swipe someone else's intellectual property. If you choose a title and see it's in use, then get creative and pick something different. Language is a beautiful and malleable tool. Bend it how you like to get the best title and subtitle choice that makes sense and can get search traffic.

Before we get any further, you must follow Amazon guidelines when it comes to keyword use. For title and subtitle choice, avoid trade-marked names and using other people's intellectual property. For back end keywords, never use any Amazon-based name such as:

- Amazon
- Amazon Prime
- Kindle Unlimited
- And more!

And, the big one is the "F" word – free. Unless your book has context for the word free (and it's not the price of your book), do not use free in your backend keywords. "Dairy-free" or "gluten-free" are examples of when free is allowed. However, Amazon has been known to unwittingly push back on publishers for using "free" in their backend keywords. Sadly, you'll have to state your case and add context as to why you have the "F" word in your keyword slots.

Now that you have a title and subtitle fleshed out, it's time to put some of the other keywords to use in your description. Many would-be experts have long touted that book descriptions are not indexed on Amazon. But, that's the furthest thing from the truth. The process of indexing is when a site places an item as searchable. Just because you have an unheard-of keyword in your description and you can't pull it up in incognito search does not prove book descriptions aren't indexed.[2]

Furthermore, if Amazon didn't index their book descriptions, then at the very least, you would have to account for the end-user – the browsing customer. What better way to validate a browsing customer's search by including keywords relevant to their needs? Organically and tastefully, weave about six to twelve keywords into your description. If you can't get six, that's okay. An excellent book description doesn't always need the best keywords. What it needs is good ad copy that has the browsing customer reading from top to bottom. After reading your excellent description, they should be dying to buy your book.

Keyword Selection + BISAC Choice = Category Placement

When uploading your book to KDP, you'll get to choose two different BISACs. The Book Industry Standards and Communications (BISAC) categories are the internationally accepted categorization for books.[3]

Amazon loosely uses BISAC to help categorize their publications on their platform. If you search the Amazon Marketplace, you won't see a single BISAC category. Why? Because Amazon has its own ways of categorizing. Its categories are there to serve the customer and create a better shopping experience.

Based on the keywords in your book's metadata and the BISAC selection, Amazon then automatically slips your book into categories exclusive to the website. Typically, a category, also known as a browse path, is a mixture of keywords and BISAC, hence why Amazon automatically slips your book into three different browse paths. Behind the scenes, the browse path looks like this:

Kindle Store > Health, Fitness & Dieting > Exercise & Fitness > Ab Workouts

However, the customer-facing category is typically a keyword term describing it like:

Ab Workouts (Kindle Store)

When you go to a book's product page and scroll down to the product details, you'll see the category selection. Click on it to be redirected to the Amazon Bestseller's list for that category. If you don't see any categories in the product details, then the book hasn't had any sales.

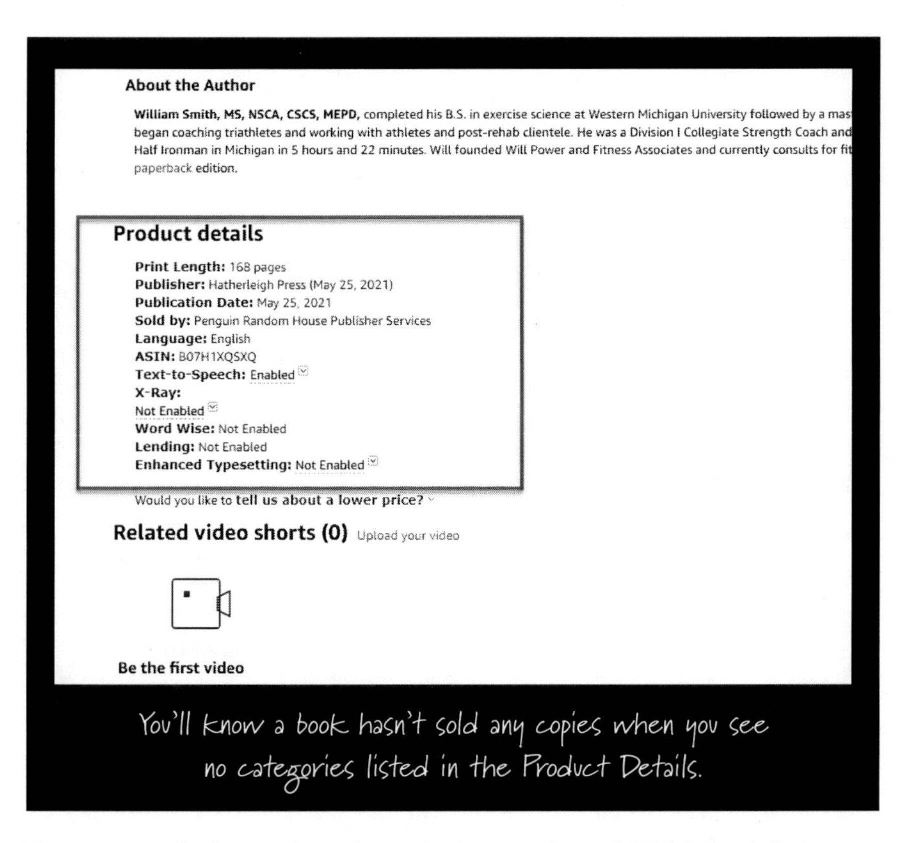

You'll know a book hasn't sold any copies when you see no categories listed in the Product Details.

Bear in mind, if you select the right keywords and BISAC while having a specific type of book, then your book could qualify for invite-only categories. For instance, if you have a short book, you could be eligible for Amazon Short Reads. Again, it's invite-only. However, you can ask to be added to those categories. The worst Amazon can say is no.

Fun fact: I covered Amazon Kindle Short Reads extensively on YouTube. Check out a full video series at DaleLinks.com/ShortReads.

How Do You Fill the Seven Keyword Slots?

After being in the business for over six years, I finally reviewed old titles I published to assess the metadata. Every book needs a good look over and polishing after being on the market for a while. Heck, even the Harry Potter books get a cover change and different descriptions. Your books are no different. I'd recommend evaluating your books more frequently than every six years.

I'm embarrassed to admit I have quite a few titles I haven't touched since my first year in the business. When I reviewed them, I discovered my use of KDP's seven keyword slots was a complete missed opportunity. Each one of the seven slots had one-term keywords - all that space and no real direction.

If you didn't skip forward in the book, then you'll know using single-term keywords for discoverability is not a good idea. You have to expand your keyword phrase and niche down to find your exact audience.

Kindle Direct Publishing allows you seven keyword slots with up to fifty characters per slot. The browsing customer will never see these backend keywords, but hopefully, they'll see your book as a result of using these keywords. These seven keyword slots are a direct line to the Amazon algorithm and a way for you to communicate to it what your book is about. Get it right, and the algorithm will have confidence in your book and build relevance around your selected keywords. Get it wrong, and your book will languish in obscurity.

Not to be confused, the seven keyword slots aren't the be-all, end-all. They're just one metric the algorithm uses in determining the relevancy of your title. This is a missed opportunity for so many authors publishing through KDP.

What do you put in these keyword slots? We already know what you shouldn't put into them, so let's shift gears into what you should put in. Remember your list of vetted keywords? Well, it's time to put those to use.

First, avoid putting your title and subtitle in the seven keyword slots. That's just redundant and won't garner you more search volume. Heck, even KDP says so on their help page.[4] If you have a shared root keyword and build a keyword derivative from the title and subtitle, then that's fine. I encourage you to use different descriptors to get better chances of more comprehensive placement across the platform.

From your list, identify the winners and earmark those for placement in the seven slots. If you found a particularly good keyword with low product results and middle of the road ABSR, then hang onto that for something special.

Find keywords that have overlap. You're looking for keywords with similar root keywords or a shared keyword of sorts. As an example:

- Home workout
- Workout plan
- Exercise plan
- Workout for men

These all share something in common, so I'm going to see if I can build a broad keyword match. Hey, remember the old broad keyword match we talked about towards the beginning of this book? Yep, here's where it's applicable.

The theory is the Amazon algorithm uses the keywords in your seven slots, but it doesn't exclusively rely on exact matches. It focuses more on a broad keyword match. So, this means we can combine a few keywords with similarities in one spot to maximize the little space we have. Then, the algorithm will decipher the words and pick out what makes the most sense to the browsing customer.

In the previous example, we could create one keyword slot from the 4 keywords to read:

Home workout exercise plan for men

That's not too bad since it has a total of thirty-four out of fifty characters used. We might be able to squeeze in more if it made sense. What you don't want to do is fill the slot with a bunch of unrelated, nonsensical words. That may just confuse the algorithm and waste your slot.

Dave Chesson of Kindlepreneur.com shared a case study where he worked with several books published through KDP. In the study, he ran tests on the seven keyword slots over some time to determine the efficacy of filling a slot versus using exact matches. He concluded that four to six slots were best served as filled to the brim. While the other one to three slots should be an exact match. He did not determine if the order made any difference, so all bets are off there.[5]

So, go through your keyword list:

1. Identify your winners – select about one to three keywords for exact matches.

2. Find overlapping keywords.

3. Combine keywords with overlap for a total of four to six keyword slots.

The most important thing is to review your keywords at least once per year. If sales are going well, then leave them alone. If book sales are horrible after ninety days, then re-evaluate your choices and switch out a few.

The hardest part of choosing and sticking to your keywords is not knowing whether the algorithm deems your book relevant to those keywords. Yes, you can build relevancy with impressions, clicks, buys, and engagement, but how much is enough? Sadly, these are factors outside of our control. The best solution to the lack of relevancy is marketing and promotion. Send more eyes to your product page and get more action going on there. This is a never-ending task, and there's never a day where you can sit back and relax.

Do you ever see brands like Nike, McDonald's, or Coca-Cola stop advertising? No. They pump millions of dollars into advertising, all to continue to be relevant in today's marketplace. The same will go for you as an author. Even cash-strapped authors have options in guest appearances, interviews, in-store signings, speaking engagements, and more. So, no one is immune to doing the work to gain more relevance for their book.

Do not spend every waking hour of your time searching for your book in incognito mode. Just as a reminder, you may not be able to find your book through incognito mode. That doesn't mean someone else isn't seeing your book in their search results. Relax and let the algorithm do its work. You should be worried about promoting your current book and writing your next. Don't sweat an algorithm you have zero control over.

I have one big piece of advice here: keywords don't sell books. Keywords merely make your book more discoverable, that's it! If you have a trash cover and a horrible book description, then no one is going to buy it.

You need to set your ego aside for a minute while I tell you this next piece of advice. If your book isn't selling, it's not an Amazon problem. It's a you problem.

Amazon wants you to succeed and has given you every free tool imaginable to make it happen. If you aren't getting sales, then it comes down to something fundamentally wrong with your book. And, keywords only make up a fraction of the reason why. With millions of customers on the market, I'm hard-pressed in believing your book was never served to several customers on a given day. Facts. It's just a numbers game, and if you aren't selling, then you aren't playing right.

If your book was selling like gangbusters at one point, but has nearly come to a halt, then it's time for you to reassess your keywords, your metadata, and your cover. I'd recommend at the soonest, you change all that out within ninety days. At minimum, assess your keywords once per year. If you have high sales, then leave it alone; you're on the right track.

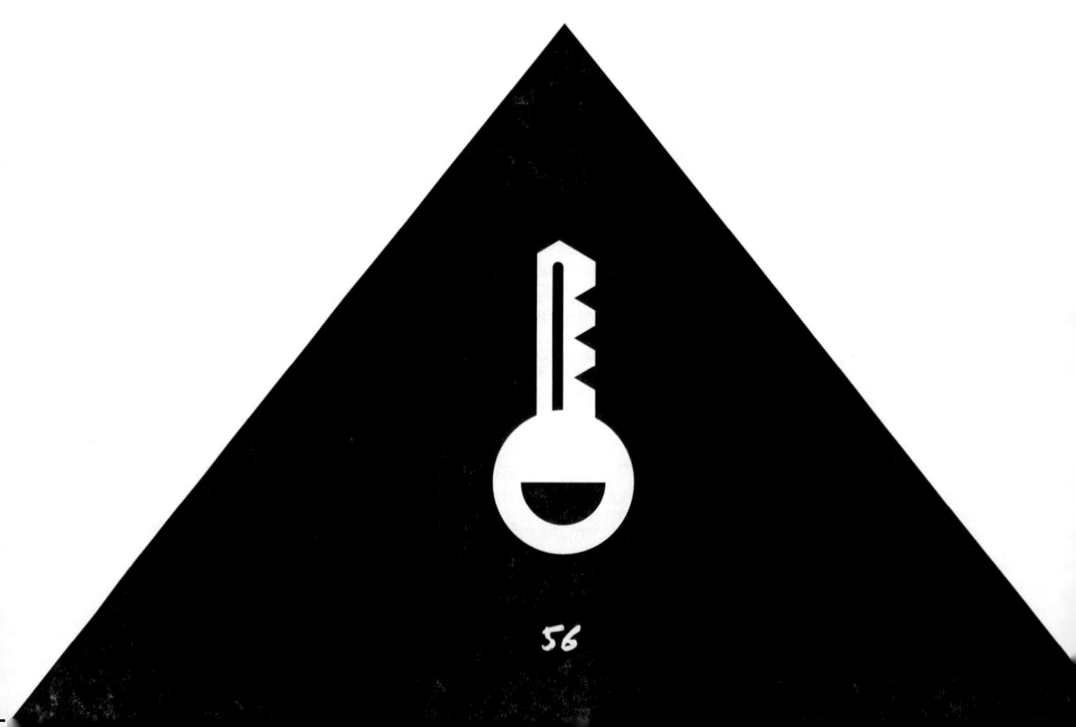

Keywords ▾

Leveraging Amazon Ads for Better Keywords

Before diving deep into leveraging the Amazon Advertising platform, it's a good idea we lay the groundwork and set some expectations. I won't be teaching you how to run Amazon Advertising campaigns. There are far more qualified experts you can learn from, so I'll send you to some excellent resources in the back of this book.

Next, do *not* invest any money you cannot stand to lose when advertising. If you're new to advertising, be prepared to lose money upfront. I'm not telling you to just throw money away so you can learn through osmosis. It just doesn't work that way. You'll need to learn from your mistakes and study the data. Running ads requires a highly analytical mind and patience.

The best way to look at advertising is you're going to pay to learn for the first year or so. Once you understand the fundamentals of advertising, you can begin to expand on your knowledge and scale your ads for more discoverability. Just don't expect it to happen over the next few weeks.

The best rule to follow when it comes to Amazon Advertising is to start low and scale slow. Your keyword bids need to be absurdly low (around 10₵ to 15₵ per click), and your daily budget should be nearly the same (around $1 to $10 per day). If you cannot afford to lose $30 to $300 per month, then you shouldn't be fooling with ads. Period.

But, stay with me throughout this chapter, even if you are cash-strapped and Amazon Advertising isn't an option. Amazon Advertising is the most underutilized tool when it comes to uncovering hidden gems and building relevancy. Amazon ads are nearly unparalleled.

When you start to advertise, begin by running a research ad. You'll want to have at least 100 keywords with a maximum of 1,000 keywords. I like to have wiggle room in case I find an exact phrase that I want to add to the campaign. So, I'll usually start an ad campaign above 500 keywords but below 900 total. Then, I can add keywords on an ad as it gains traction.

Your ad should start getting impressions in the first week. The beautiful part is impressions come free. Yep, they're showing your book to the browsing customers for free. Remember, those "Sponsored" book placements in the search results? That's one of many places where it will appear.

Not everyone will pay mind to your ad. The good thing is Amazon Advertising will place your book in front of people. And, one could assume this ad will appear in front of the same person repeatedly. Then, your book cover image and title will work it's way into their subconscious. Eventually, they'll either have to see what you're book is all about or circle back around and search for your book again to purchase it. Pretty neat, right?

It's very much like what Tai Lopez did on YouTube about four or five years ago with his "in my garage with my Lamborgini" video ad. He placed that ad in front of millions of people, and quite a few people (myself included), skipped his ad. It served only as an impression on YouTube Ads. But, after being interrupted so many times, I finally watched the ad in its entirety. Now, I doubt I bought any of his products as a result, but it goes to show he left a lasting impression on me and built his massive online presence through this dumb yet ingenious video ad.

The same can work for you, except without having to flex with your Lambo on customers. These impressions add up over time. It's when you get the clicks that it makes the most difference.

For my research ads, I typically go with broad keyword matches. Once I start getting clicks, the cost will be low, but I'll be able to see what works and what doesn't for my title. Once you get clicks, monitor your "Search Terms" report. It'll show you precisely what the customer searched to get your book as an ad. If you see a keyword that doesn't convert well, you can add it to your negative phrases, so your ad isn't served to anyone using that term again.

Amazon Advertising more recently rolled out the "Search Terms" feature in each ad campaign.

Conversely, if a keyword converts to a sale, then you need to start building derivative keywords on it in your campaign at the same bid to see if you get more sales. More specifically, you want to take the exact match of the keyword the customer used to convert a purchase and add it to your campaign. Set that keyword as an exact match and bid about 2₵ to 5₵ higher than what it converted at, so long as you are not losing money on the bidding.

A common misconception is if you bid higher on a keyword, you'll get first-page placement. That's simply not true. It comes down to relevancy again. Amazon Advertising will choose the ad that best fits for relevancy, not on the bid alone.

As an example, you have a book selling fifteen copies per day, and I have a book selling one copy per day. You bid 15₵ on a given keyword, while I bid 75₵ on the same keyword. At that given moment, your bid is going to win because your book is a proven commodity. I won't have to pay the 75₵ thankfully, since the winning bid was 15₵. I'll automatically bid below that amount.

Once you understand how Amazon Advertising is like a live auction with clout-based rules, you'll be able to realistically scale. This is why I always recommend you start low and scale slow.

With Amazon Ads, you're going to find some keywords that you win every time. Those are the keywords you should pay the closest attention to and consider using in your metadata if you haven't already. I've found some real gems and seen my sales bump up when adding some of these high-converting keywords. The exceptions to this advice are, of course, author names, trademark names, brands, and the like. Though you can use them in ad campaigns, you still cannot use it in your book's metadata.

If you find a keyword that isn't converting at all and leads to no sales, then make sure to remove it from your book's metadata. It's clearly indicating the audience who uses this keyword in search does not resonate with your product page. Kill it in your description and remove it from your seven keyword slots. It's dead weight.

I highly recommend reading through the Amazon Advertising FAQs[6] and Help[7] section to get a better grasp on how the platform functions best. Also, study Google Ads for a better understanding of how keywords and ads work together.

Amazon Advertising continues to tweak its platform and incorporate a lot of Google Ads principles. One way is how Google does the auction-based system. Google ranks an ad based on a quality score. The way Google scores an ad is based on the landing page experience, the expected click-through rate (number of clicks to impressions), and ad relevance. They further score the quality based on the keywords in the ad, the domain name, and the landing page.[8]

Ultimately, Google will place an ad based on the bid, the quality, and format impact. All that to say, it's not just a platform that sells to the highest bidder. Much in the way Google wants its customers to have a good browsing experience, Amazon wants the same for their customers.

If Amazon doesn't have much confidence in your book, then the ad may not get served often. But, as your book gets more sales and better conversions, then Amazon is more apt to place your ad in a prominent area. And, it's not always about who is willing to pay the highest dollar. Though when it comes to pound-for-pound relevancy, bidding is the next most important metric.

Using Amazon Advertising puts you at a significant advantage over those who do not. You'll get a peek into what customers are searching for and what lead them to become your reader. You're less blind to the customer's journey on Amazon prior to them buying your book. If knowledge is power, then Amazon Advertising is equipping you with the data you need to become a more powerful publisher. Don't take it lightly or for granted.

But, don't hedge all your bets on Amazon Advertising. If you're currently using the platform and losing hundreds on it, then take a step back and study it a bit more. You're probably missing something. I'd recommend reaching out to other peers in this industry who use Amazon ads. Mastermind options and ways to optimize your campaigns. Because, who likes to simply flush money down the drain? I know I don't, and nor should you.

Keywords ▾

Building Keyword Relevancy

How exactly do you build relevancy on your title then? We've covered quite a few ways to build relevancy for your title, but it bears worth in repeating. If you can master these ways, then you're off to a better start than most people. Rather than repeating myself, it's best to interweave other tips to build search engine optimization you may have never thought about doing.

The number one way to build relevancy is sales. Nothing builds Amazon's confidence in your product more than cold, hard sales. Anyone who thinks Amazon is merely a political game or how they're favoring only individual books are misled. In an age when ABDL (adult baby diaper lover) absolutely dominates, I can confidently say most any book can. Sure, there are limitations, and you can find out more about the content that KDP does not want you publishing on its platform. Some books simply cannot use Amazon ad campaigns due to their adult nature.

Beyond those few limitations, you should know Amazon wants you to win. After all, if you win, they win. You make money, they make money. But, it can't be an entirely one-sided give and take relationship. What you're willing to take, you have to give somewhat. That's why you cannot merely expect to publish and pray for Amazon to make it a success. Fat freakin' chance. Even *this* book isn't immune to that.

So, what drives sales better than more sales? How do you get more sales? Marketing and promoting. And you must never stop. This is an on-going process that works in perpetuity. You never stop marketing.

One of the best places to advertise is Amazon itself. That's why I'm incredibly bullish about using the Amazon Advertising platform. When using Facebook Ads or Google Ads, you're initially dealing with a cold audience with few exceptions. You're meeting them on another platform where you have to redirect them to your product.

With Amazon, you have a warm audience who are coming to spend money on products. When a customer arrives on Amazon, they're not going to be put off by ads. Why? Because that's all the platform is. It's mostly a search engine that delivers people to products. Amazon has gotten good at interweaving ads in a way that appears seamless. The only indication of it being an ad is where it says "Sponsored." Most customers and outsiders don't even know what that label means.

What it means to you is a customer who's primarily searching for a solution to their problem. Where you'd typically only have your book served for a limited keyword set, you have 1,000 keywords in an Amazon ad. Wow! Who needs seven keyword slots when you are allowed 1,000 keywords in an ad campaign?

As shared before, you don't have to spend hundreds per day to have your book in front of readers. You can start out as low as $1 per day. That's less than the cost of a Starbucks Coffee. I'll pass on the caffeine if that means my book will get in front of people for the next few days.

Will Amazon ads build relevancy for your title? Absolutely. But, it will *not* be the answer to all of your sales problems. If your book has a horrible cover and description, then no ad is going to help solve the issue. Let's face it, selling any product is a numbers game. No matter how ugly your product is or how bad the ad copy, every now and then, you'll get a sale. Your book will hit some customer at the right time who'll forgive a bad cover and won't care about your mistake-riddled book description.

But, what did it take to convert that one sale? How many impressions did it take? How many clicks after that? What is the ratio of impressions to clicks to buys? If it's a lop-sided ratio where you're only converting one in every one-million impressions, then you have an issue.

Amazon Ads are merely plugging a leak in your boat. Sure, every blind squirrel gets a nut once in a while, you cannot view that as the norm. I can guarantee once you stop advertising, your book will go back to languishing in obscurity. That's why it's paramount to pay close attention to the data. Customers will tell you if your book is worth a darn. If it's not selling despite perceived relevant keywords, then you've got a book problem that needs addressing before you can expect better results from your campaigns.

The one time when Amazon Advertising builds more relevancy on your title is when the book is already doing well. It's selling copies like crazy! So, then you add advertising to the mix and boom! You're then running on all cylinders and cooking on all burners.

Speaking of cooking with gas, one of the best ways to enjoy a meal is in the company of friends. And, naturally, when you go to launch your book, you may ask your friends and family to grab it. If you're going against my previous recommendations about friends and family, then I'm going to at least equip you with an easy way to build relevancy.

Instead of sending friends and family to your product page through a link, tell them a keyword, your author name, or the title of your book. Have them visit Amazon to pick up your book with that information.

Yes, you're sending them on a wild goose chase. However, if they're going to be doing your evil bidding, you might as well have them help in search engine optimization.

You could do the same thing when it comes to followers, but I wouldn't recommend it. Don't annoy them or lose out on a potential sale because you wanted to build relevancy for your title.

Sending customers to Amazon equipped with the right keywords to find your book will have them acting like an average browsing customer and selecting your book based on keywords. For every time someone searches for a given keyword, finds your title, and purchases it, that's another action aiding in relevancy.

A few ways to send your readers is by:

- A specific keyword you want to build relevancy for
- Your title and/or subtitle
- Your author name – don't take this lightly. Eventually, you'll build enough relevancy your author name will appear in autosuggest. If you're already published, see if you're appearing there already.

The biggest issue in sending people this way is the fall off. A lot of people don't want to jump through hoops and would rather go right to your page. And, some people won't get the impetus behind you wanting to build more relevance in a search engine. All they hear is, "Me, me, me, me, me…oh, and by the way, me."

It's a big enough task for someone to look for your book, let alone look at it, that it can be a rather tall order asking for them to search for it.

If you do send them on a hunt for your book, at least show them what the cover looks like, so they aren't getting lost. Again, you don't want to frustrate your potential readers. This is why I say this method almost always works out better for friends and family. They're a bit more forgiving.

For followers on social media or subscribers to your email list, give them the link. Don't play around. They just want to get your book and be done with it. Toying with their emotions isn't a good idea. They're bound to wait to get your book another day, if at all. So, give them a direct link.

Never use the long link created from a search on Amazon. Go into your KDP dashboard, find your book, select the region in the drop-down for the publication, and then go there. Use that short link. It'll probably be something like:

https://www.amazon.com/dp/B0197JK7Z2

You want everyone to buy your book when they visit your product page. That's what will build relevancy. And, if you can, try to be deliberate about when and where you ask. Sending a ton of traffic all at once is suitable for the short term. Still, the algorithm favors consistent performing products versus the short-term trending product. Trickle the traffic, and you'll see much better results.

The next best action to build relevancy is getting more reviews. Review gathering should be part of your regular marketing and promotion strategy. Also, you should add a call-to-action at the end of every book for readers to leave a review on Amazon.

In fact, here's the easiest way to send readers directly to the review page:

> https://www.amazon.com/gp/product-review/(ADD YOUR BOOK ASIN HERE)

You merely have to add your ebook or print book's ASIN/ISBN at the end of the link, then you're set. When you first launch your ebook, you won't have an ASIN. So, you'll have to wait until it's launched to insert the full call-to-action. When asking for a review, keep it simple, and do not try to influence their response. Keep it cut and dry like:

> Now that you finished reading the book, it'd mean the world to me if you left an honest review on Amazon at (INSERT LINK).

You could add some pizazz to that; however, you get the idea.

I'd recommend sharing posted reviews on social media, in your newsletter, and in future books. Follow it up with a simple call-to-action like the previous one. You could say something simple like:

> Have you read (INSERT YOUR TITLE HERE)? If so, it'd mean the world to me if you left an honest review on Amazon at (INSERT LINK). Reviews like this one and yours help me to better craft books and content, so I can make a bigger impact in the world.

The last part was just a random way to share what's in it for them. Plus, it gives permission to your reader to drop feedback and your receptiveness to using it to produce better content.

You'd be amazed at how well this works for low reviews. If you see a one-star review and share it with your following, they'll be quick to drop better reviews to balance out the bad. It's nothing I'd recommend you purposely coordinate since Amazon doesn't like coercion or bias. However, it's definitely a great indirect way to balance out your reviews while building relevancy on your product page.

Of course, remember you can always respond to all book reviews. Keep it professional. Don't respond to some of them and ignore the rest. If you're going to do some, then address all of them. Just don't get defensive.

You get bonus points if you can somehow organically weave in keywords relevant to your book. This is just another way to index your title and validate customer search. It's double bonus points when your readers post a review with your keyword. Again, don't coerce them. That's not a good idea.

The next way to increase relevancy is by asking for friends, family, and followers to share your book through the social media link from your product page. These small social triggers are enough to create small signals to the algorithm and it builds a bit more confidence in your product. One great feature product pages have is the embed feature. You can take a sample from the book and embed it on a website page. This is yet another way to send more traffic to your book.

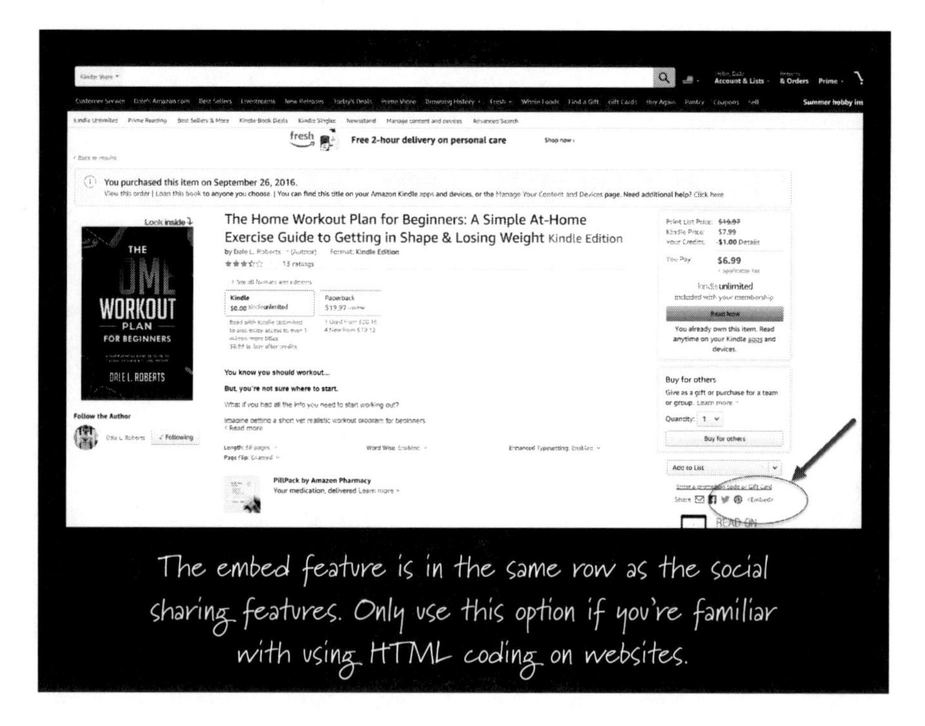

The embed feature is in the same row as the social sharing features. Only use this option if you're familiar with using HTML coding on websites.

The second most underutilized tool by authors on Amazon is the lists feature. Let your followers know that it's totally okay if they aren't able to buy your books right now. The best way for them to help out and support the cause is by adding your book to a wish list. The nice part is, if they make the wish list public, someone might buy the book for them.

Getting your book added to a list on Amazon helps in your book being placed in additional categories, one of them being "Gift Ideas." You'll most notably see this category surface around the holidays. Do not take this option lightly.

Another highly underutilized tool by authors on Amazon is Author Central. Amazon equips authors with a profile page at no additional cost. And, the beautiful part is this page is another way to index your books and share from one spot. So, rather than sending your followers to any one book's product page, you can send them to your Amazon Author Profile.

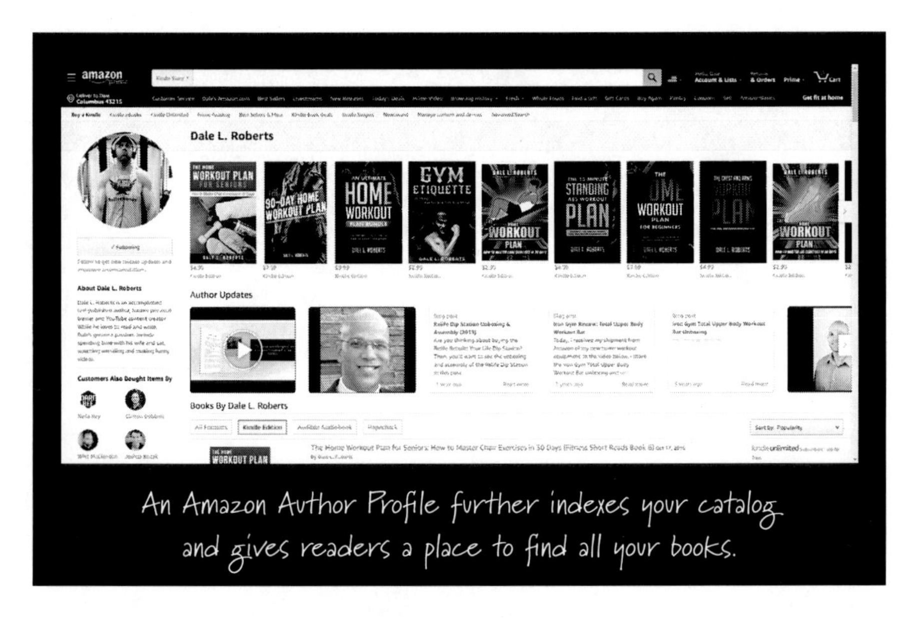

An Amazon Author Profile further indexes your catalog and gives readers a place to find all your books.

Also, having an Amazon Author Profile makes your author name a clickable link on your book's page. Once a customer clicks on your author name, they'll be whisked away to your author profile where they'll get to see other books by you. This, in turn, builds more awareness of your other titles. There's also a sweet little "Follow" button located below your author picture. When a visitor clicks on that, Amazon will notify them when you release your next book. Though the notifications are a bit delayed, it still helps for little bursts of sales after a book launch.

Author Central has several neat features, but the biggest ones include: all your reviews curated in one spot, editorial reviews, and historical sales ranking. The latter option is useful if you obsessively camp out on your product page. If you do camp out there, I'd recommend you move to Author Central. The issue with hitting refresh on your book's page is it slowly erodes the relevancy of your title since you are not buying the book. Though this is merely a theory, it's not one I'm willing to test since Author Central tracks your Amazon Bestseller Rank.

> Fun fact: A few years ago, I shared a comprehensive overview of Amazon Author Central. Take a look at the video series at DaleLinks.com/AuthorCentral.

One last way to build relevancy is an indirect feature made available through the magic of Amazon. It's the "Also Bought" and "Frequently Bought Together" features on a product page.

Amazon customers are notorious for buying more than one product per transaction. So, Amazon made it simple for other customers to see what previous customers have bought in tandem. Nothing attracts a crowd like a crowd. When other customers notice another product was purchased along with the current product they're considering, they're apt to either:

A. Check out the other product – if that other product is your book, yay! If not, boo hiss!
B. Buy both products.

Quite a few customers used to buy a number of my fitness books together or with other fitness author's books.

You typically will only see this feature on products that have been on Amazon for a while. This is not a feature you'll see on the first day of launch or during pre-orders. Why? Because Amazon is stating a fact when it says these items are frequently bought together.

You'll find the "Customers Who Bought This Item Also Bought" and a row of selections on most ebook listings. For print books, it'll say

"Frequently Bought Together" where it'll show your print book listed with other print books including a total cost of both together.

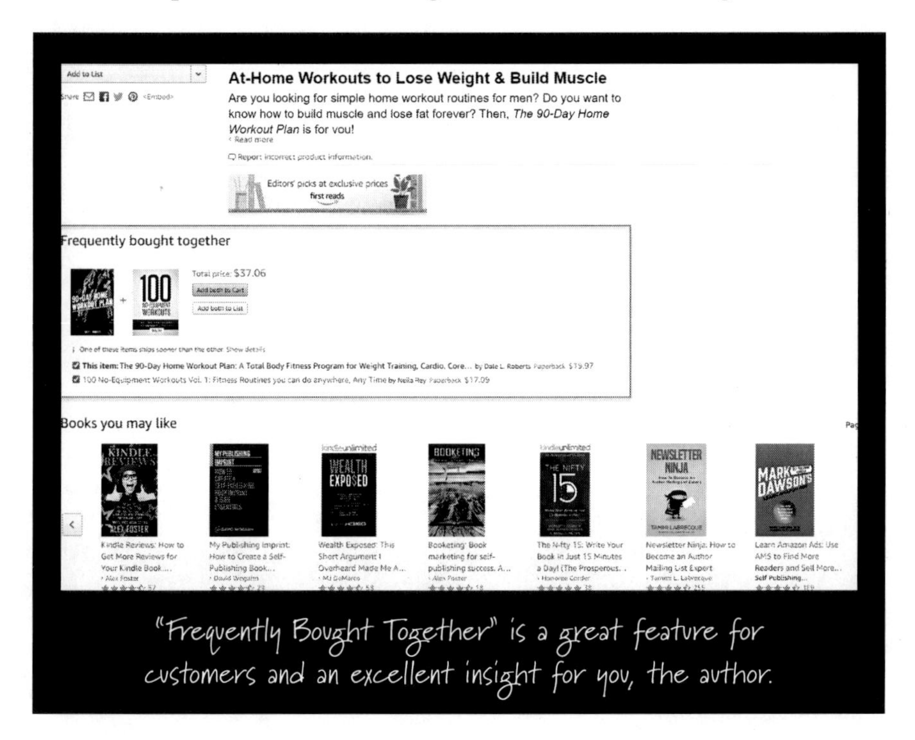

"Frequently Bought Together" is a great feature for customers and an excellent insight for you, the author.

"Also Bought" and "Frequently Bought Together" is why I discourage marketing and promoting to friends and family. Unless you have someone close who is your ideal reader (sorry, your mom doesn't count), asking them to buy your books is going to mess up this feature. It just confuses the algorithm, and if you do it bad enough, you'll end up in some weird combinations.

Will it kill your relevancy having friends and family buying your books? It's certainly debatable. Rather than be saddled with the heartache of cleaning up your "Also Boughts" and rebuilding your book's relevancy, it's best to err on the side of caution.

Is there any one thing that could kill relevancy for your book? Yes. Complacency. I can assure you after allowing my fitness brand to sit unattended for over three years, those books' better days are behind them. Though it was not my sole source of income, it was undoubtedly the main contributor in my early publishing days. If I had to do it all over again, I would've assigned a manager to promote those assets. That would've mitigated any loss in relevancy.

I'd recommend the same to you. To maintain a strong foothold on Amazon, you need to have a consistent marketing and promotion plan to keep your book's relevancy high.

When you're hard-pressed on running ads, then follow the old adage prolific author and co-host of 20BooksTo50K, Craig Martelle says:

> Nothing sells your last book like the next book.[9]

So, when forced to do the next best thing, write your next book and keep pushing forward.

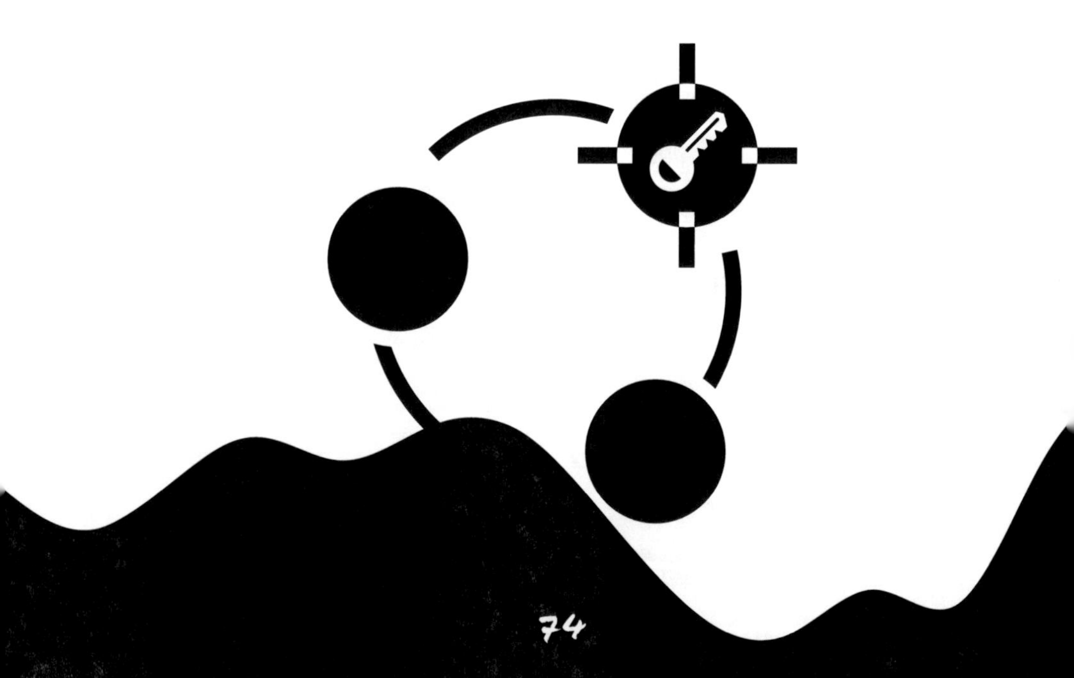

Keywords ▾

Keyword Tools & Resources

Well, now that you learned it all the hard way, I'm going to give you a few ideas for tools to consider to add to your arsenal. Some tools come at a premium, and others don't cost a dime. Of course, some of my preferred tools are free, but I have one that I don't go without, and it does cost a premium.

Publisher Rocket

Publisher Rocket is a premium tool with four different features: Competition Analysis, Category Research, and the two most essential tools, the AMS Keywords Finder, and the Keyword Research Tool. The last two options alone are worth the $97 investment I made three years ago.

Rather than spend hours trawling about on Amazon for relevant keywords, Publisher Rocket does it all in a matter of minutes. And, the best part about Rocket, is how you see the estimated number of searches per month and a competition score. Getting to see the estimated searches per month is a game-changer, and it gives you a better overview of how a keyword performs beyond just the ABSR, number of products, shelf-life, and reviews.

The second feature, the AMS Keywords Finder, makes creating Amazon Advertising campaigns a cinch. You simply type in a keyword relevant to your title, and Rocket comes back with hundreds of relevant keywords. My best campaigns were run using the Rocket AMS Keywords Finder.

I'd recommend if you use this feature for ads, grab your seven backend keywords to build a list. If you have to break down some keyword combinations, do that before you run a report with Rocket.

Believe it or not, this book went through three different versions. This version is the product of a complete overhaul and rewrite. In the last two versions, I leaned heavily into how much I loved this tool. But, I was afraid it'd turn off readers and make them believe it was merely a book meant to sell Publisher Rocket licenses.

When reflecting on my career over the past six years, the first three years I went without any tools. Yeah, the first two years were tough as hell, but if it weren't for learning the fundamentals of keywords, I wouldn't be able to share the information in this book nor carve out a career as an indie author.

So, rather than gushing over Publisher Rocket anymore, I'd recommend you watch my video review about the product at DaleLinks.com/RocketReview so you get a better overview. Or, you can head to my affiliate link at DaleLinks.com/Rocket for more details.

Kindlepreneur

Okay, I'm not gonna lie. You could literally throw this book in the trash in front of me if you agreed to go straight to Kindlepreneur.com. This is one of the best resources online today when it comes to understanding the business of self-publishing! Run by indie author and self-publishing expert, Dave Chesson, Kindlepreneur is the self-publisher's self-publisher. When indie authors have a problem, they typically reach out to Dave for the answer.

Flip to the back of the book to get a full list of articles I find the most informative. Any post written by Dave is meticulous and well crafted while staying simple enough to read in one sitting.

DS Amazon Quick View

This Chrome browser extension is a godsend and doesn't have to cost a dime. Heck, I've used the free version for the past couple of years and don't know how I functioned without it. Remember, how I had you painstakingly research your keywords and click on each product page to scroll to the product details for the ABSR, publication date, and reviews? Well, you get to see that all in the search results.

Before you start researching next time, install DS Amazon Quick View into your browser. Then, enable the browser extension for incognito mode. Simply go to your browser settings, then go to your extensions. Now, find DS Amazon Quick View. Then, enable it for incognito mode.

You're all set then. Next time you're doing research, you'll see a gray box below the books in the search results. It'll show the ABSR. Hover your mouse over top of the book cover to reveal the product details.

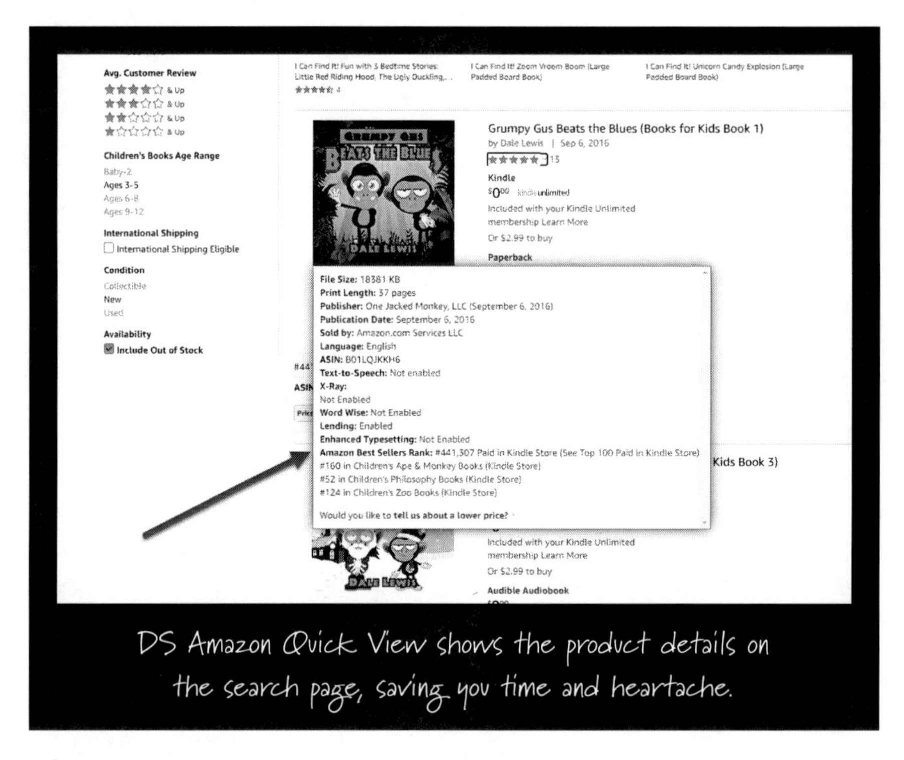

DS Amazon Quick View shows the product details on the search page, saving you time and heartache.

DS Amazon Quick View is simply the best tool you can find for considerably shortening your keyword research time. Sorry in advance if you did hours of research only to discover this option. Again, I didn't want to seem like a complete shill for all these products.

Understanding Search Engines

If you really want to master the game of self-publishing and keyword use, then you need to get a better understanding of search engine algorithms. I invested thousands into books, videos and courses to learn what I know. And, I hate to tell you, this doesn't even scratch the surface. If a search engine programmer read this book, they'd lose their mind at how much I minimized the work they put in.

The areas you'll want to focus on are Google, YouTube, Facebook, Instagram, Twitter, and of course, Amazon. Getting the right information is easier than you know. You've already made it through this book, so you clearly have the aptitude for learning about keywords. I'd assume you'd be willing to learn even more, especially if you're a self-starter.

Rather than plunking down a ton of money, I'd recommend a few free resources to start you off. First of all, YouTube is your friend and can bring you back a ton of free content. I've found some of the best free content on YouTube. Just be picky about who you learn from. If someone is flexing with their Range Rover on you, then chances are likely, they aren't trying to teach you, they're trying to fleece you. Run away. However, someone who's been in the writing community for a while may have your best interests at heart and won't give any misinformation.

Other places to grab great info is your local library. Believe it or not, there are lots of print books, ebooks, and audiobooks designed to teach you more about search engines. I'd say pick a platform and run with it. Amazon is a good place. If I'd recommend any other, it'd be Google or even YouTube next.

Also, some libraries are enrolled in a course platform called LinkedIn Learning formerly known as Lynda.com. If you have a library card, all you have to do is sign in with your library card, and you can get scores of free courses! It's ridiculously good and doesn't cost you a dime. The library and LinkedIn foot the cost so you can elevate your education.

You can also keep an eye on platforms like Udemy or Gumroad for free courses or digital downloads. It's funny, but I don't believe you need to invest more than just a little time and a willingness to learn when it comes to understanding search engines.

Keywords ▾ **Conclusion** 

After an hour of chatting about pro wrestling with Dan, Andru, and Mike, we dispersed and moved onto other conversations in the crowded room. I don't think any of us were anymore introverted than the other, but having that common ground gave us enough to get warmed up and the courage to chat with other people about anything else besides pro wrestling.

It's funny how the situation would've been different had the four of us not had that common ground. How would the conversation have gone? Would our random visitors have stayed longer? Or, would they have not even stopped by to chat in the first place? After all, nothing attracts a crowd like a small group of guys loudly and enthusiastically professing their love for a strange business that's been labeled "fake" by outsiders.

Imagine how stilted the conversation would've been without that common ground. What would we have talked about? Would we have all gone our separate ways and called it a day? Or, would we simply grind it out and find the right conversation in due time?

Keywords are organically woven into the fabric of conversation. We just never call them keywords. We call them interests, topics, passions, dreams, and the like. When you can draw a parallel between real life and business based around a machine, you bring a more human element that ties humans together.

After all, we're not selling books to machines. We're selling books through a machine to other human beings. When you can attach an emotion to what you're doing and acknowledge the person on the other side of the transaction, you'll both win in the end.

So, as you do your keyword research, upload your selected keywords, and run a campaign with keywords, remember you're not doing it for an algorithm. You're doing it to build a bridge between your book and your ideal reader. To better state it, you're starting a conversation with someone who shares the same interests as you. And, hopefully, you draw a crowd and grow a kinship in the process.

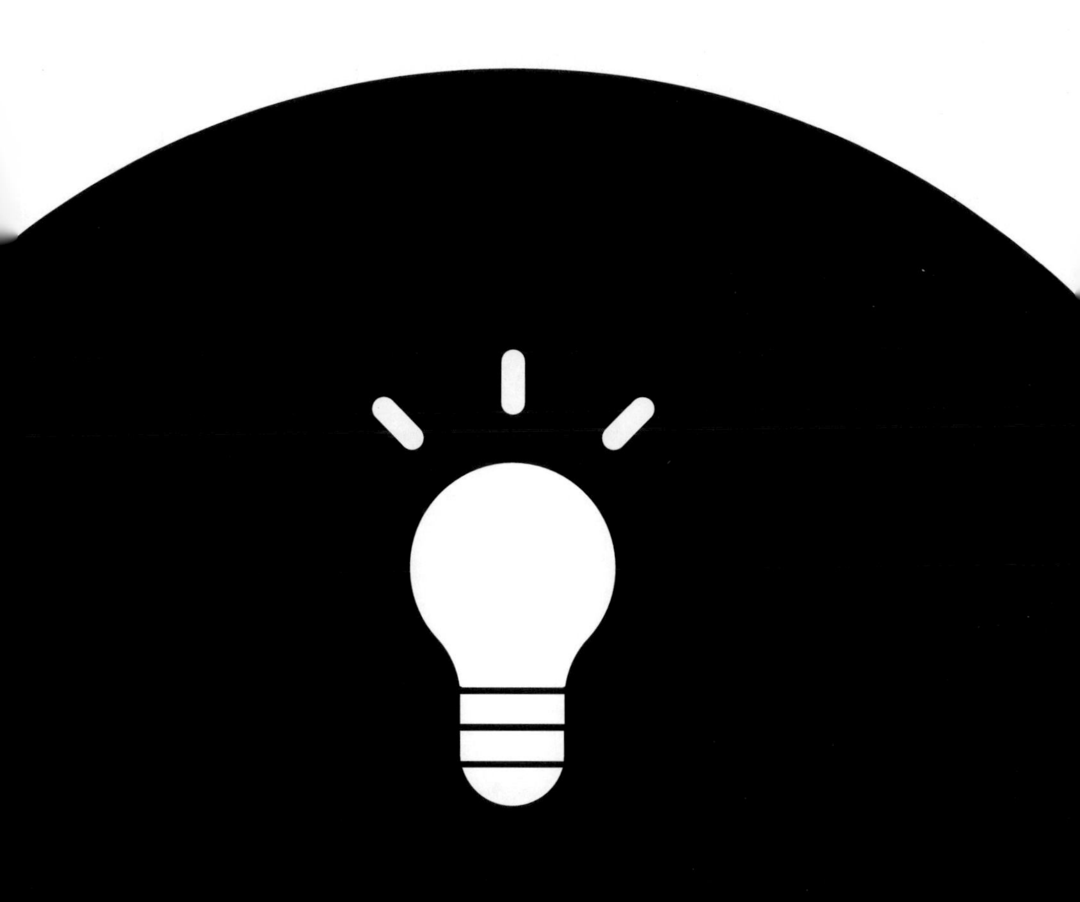

Keywords

A Small Ask...

Now that you finished reading this book, what did you think of what you read? Were there any tips or information you found insightful? What do you think was missing from this book? While you're thinking back on what you read, it'd mean the world to me if you left an honest review on Amazon.

As you know, reviews play an integral part in building relevancy for all products. So whether you found the information helpful or not, your candid review would help other customers make an informed purchase.

Also, based on your review, I'll adjust this publication and future editions. That way, you and other indie authors can learn and grow.

Feel free to leave a review at DaleLinks.com/ReviewKeywordsBook.

Keywords

About the Author

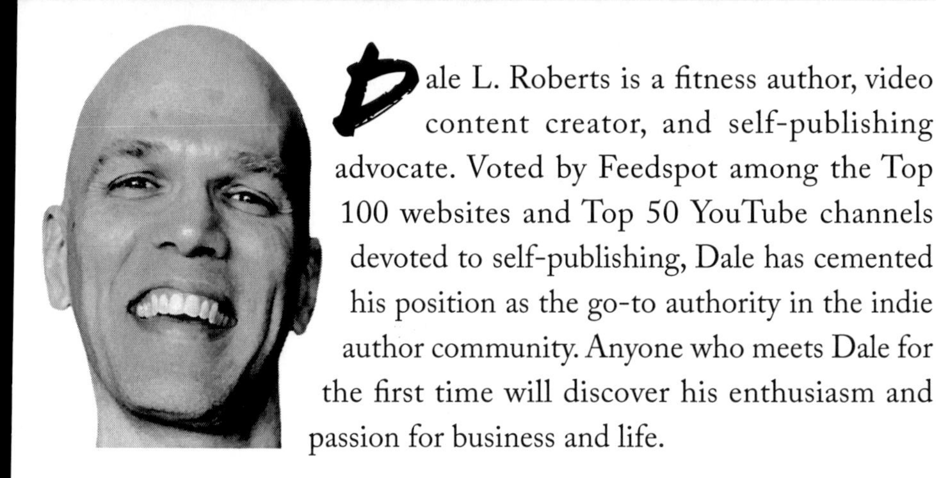

Dale L. Roberts is a fitness author, video content creator, and self-publishing advocate. Voted by Feedspot among the Top 100 websites and Top 50 YouTube channels devoted to self-publishing, Dale has cemented his position as the go-to authority in the indie author community. Anyone who meets Dale for the first time will discover his enthusiasm and passion for business and life.

When Dale isn't publishing books, creating videos, and networking with business professionals, he loves to travel with his wife Kelli and spend time playing with his cat Izzie. He currently lives in Columbus, Ohio.

Relevant links:

- Website - SelfPublishingWithDale.com
- YouTube – YouTube.com/SelfPublishingWithDale
- Twitter – Twitter.com/SelfPubWithDale
- Facebook - Facebook.com/SelfPubWithDale
- Instagram – Instagram.com/SelfPubWithDale
- DON'T GO HERE! – DaleLinks.com

Keywords ▾ Special Thanks

Holy crap, has it been nearly four years since my last fitness book? I've published quite a few other books since then, but none were under the Dale L. Roberts brand. And, in that time, I held off for a litany of reasons. My YouTube channel became a higher priority. Helping other authors also became a priority. Networking and connecting with brands and businesses became a priority. Before I knew it, four years passed, and here I was feeling anxiety and a bit of impostor syndrome. Thankfully, I had the love and support of many amazing people, including all of the following and more.

Kelli, my amazing wife, is the very reason I've doubled back around to writing again. And, when I kept saying for the past two years that I'd write a book, she decided to call me on it a few times. Well, I took massive action and wrote the whole danged first draft in one sitting in front of a live audience on my YouTube Channel.

Ava Fails, you are a truly incredible human being and I'm fortunate to have had someone as intelligent, patient, and truly beautiful in my corner for the past four years. You started working with me in the dying days of my fitness brand. And, you hung in there while things went from bad to worse for my business. Thankfully, you stuck around and we were able to get this far. I was going to leave this out because I know you all too well. You can't take a compliment. So, now you're stuck with it here, forever published for everyone to see. You aren't just the world's greatest assistant. You're also the world's most loyal and true friend.

Dan Norton, you are a gem and a bro for life. I'm inspired by your undying work ethic. You're a wellspring of ideas and a fountain of knowledge in the video creator space. Just think, we've only just started working together. Imagine what it'll look like in another year or two! Thanks for everything, bro.

Jason Bracht, I'm forever grateful for your teaching and mentoring early on. And even more thankful for your friendship. You were the best in guiding me in the right direction while others tried steering my ship into dark waters. All my success is due to the foundation you laid with me. For that, thank you.

Dave Freakin' Chesson - That's exactly how I say your name any time I see a text or call from you. You are by far the smartest guy in all of the self-publishing business. Bar none. I thank you for all your contributions to the indie author community and for being a world-class human being. And, of course, thanks for being a true friend. It means the world to me.

Michael La Ronn, you're my hero, man. I watched your videos and remember thinking if I can make my videos half as good as his, I'll have it made. I love your candid insights and always appreciate your cerebral approach to the future of this business. Stay humble and keep being you, buddy!

And, my lifelong best friend and brother, Walt. Man, you don't realize how much I've looked up to you over the years. I'm so incredibly happy to have built something again with you in the Live Streaming Tech brand. My mission is to have you out of a job and into your dream life in the next year. So, if you're reading this in 2022 and you're still in a job, I failed you. But, that ain't gonna happen, because I'm going to use this thank you message as a way to gloat about how I'm right and you're wrong. That's what brothers are for, right? Oh, and yes, I'll be singing my triumphant victory song, "I'll Always Be the Winner."

And, a big extra special thanks to my self publishing friends including, but not limited to: Keith Wheeler, Kevin Maguire, Mojo Siedlak, Scott Jay Marshall II, Mark Brownless, Al Parra Pinto, Risa Fey, Ben Gothard, Dexter Poin, Jacob Rothenberg, Su Singh, Brian Mu Lipah, Nancy O'Neill and so many more. Sorry if I missed your name. The good news is I have two other books in this series so I can get you then.

And, a big thanks to the video creator community including, but not limited to: Nick Nimmin, Brian G Johnson, Dan Currier, Gord Isman, Rob Balasabas, Andrew Kan, Dee Nimmin, Andru Edwards, Roberto Blake, Owen Video, Shannon Vlogs, Jeremy Vest, TubeBuddy, VidIQ, Nico from MorningFame, Derral Eves, Marcus Campbell, Ryan A Raymond, and so many more!

Lastly, it's important I shout-out the brands and companies who've been my biggest cheerleaders and sponsors of the Self-Publishing with Dale channel. This includes BookDoggy, Lulu, LapIt Marketing, Findaway Voices, Thinkific, Vexels, Romance Publishing Academy, Kotobee Author, Fiverr, and Winning Writers.

If I missed you in the acknowledgements and you feel you should be placed here, then feel free to fill in the blank here. Thanks, __________. Sorry, that's the best I have for now. Hit me up if you feel you should've made it in this section.

Keywords ▾ Other Notable Resources

The 5 Best Kindlepreneur Articles

1. Kindlepreneur Book Description Generator: https://dalelinks.com/html2
2. Keywords in the Book Description: https://kindlepreneur.com/keywords-in-your-book-description/
3. Sell More Books with Amazon Book Ads: https://dalelinks.com/amscourse
4. The Secret Method to Choosing Amazon Book Categories: https://dalelinks.com/choosecategories
5. +127 of the Top Free and Paid Book Promotion Sites: https://kindlepreneur.com/list-sites-promote-free-amazon-books/

The 5 Must-Read Books on Self-Publishing

1. *Mastering Amazon Ads & Mastering Amazon Descriptions* by Brian Meeks
2. *How to Write a Sizzling Synopsis* by Bryan Cohen
3. *Become a Successful Indie Author* by Craig Martelle
4. *Self-Publisher's Legal Handbook* by Helen Sedwick
5. *Successful Self-Publishing* by Joanna Penn

The 5 Must-Watch YouTube Channels Devoted to Self-Publishing

1. Book Launchers:
   https://www.youtube.com/user/julieabroad
2. Keith Wheeler Books:
   https://www.youtube.com/channel/UCcFfP0Px7cO3h6BCZUpXUQQ
3. Kindlepreneur:
   https://www.youtube.com/channel/UC-s3Pb8uIBm0QN8MVaulJKA
4. Draft2Digital:
   https://www.youtube.com/channel/UCCxkNFCpyAoQV5eAKbZwZHg
5. Author Level Up:
   https://www.youtube.com/channel/UCcdjxp-TGOOucIV1rMDS8jw

So you're ready to launch your book?

I bet you want the best book launch possible.

Of course you do!

What if you could increase your odds of hitting the Bestsellers List in your niche?

Download a copy of my *Bestseller Book Launch Checklist*…

Go, sign up!

DaleLinks.com/Checklist

Start your action plan to a better book launch right now!

Keywords ▾ **References**

1 Chesson, Dave. (n.d.) KINDLE KEYWORD RANKING PERCENTAGES: #1 VS. #2. Kindlepreneur.com. https://kindlepreneur.com/kindle-keyword-ranking-percentages-1-vs-2/

2 Chesson, Dave. (May 29, 2020) KEYWORDS IN YOUR BOOK DESCRIPTION: DO THEY HELP? Kindlepreneur.com. https://kindlepreneur.com/keywords-in-your-book-description/

3 Book Industry Study Group. (n.d.) BISAC Subject Codes FAQ. Book Industry Standard Group. https://bisg.org/page/BISACFaQ

4 Kindle Direct Publishing. (n.d.) Make Your Book More Discoverable with Keywords. Kindle Direct Publishing. https://kdp.amazon.com/en_US/help/topic/G201298500

5 Chesson, Dave. (n.d.) 7 KINDLE KEYWORDS: USE ALL 50 CHARACTERS OR NOT? Kindlepreneur.com https://kindlepreneur.com/7-kindle-keywords/

6 Amazon.com, Inc. (n.d.) FAQ. Advertising.amazon.com. https://advertising.amazon.com/resources/faq

7 Amazon.com, Inc. (n.d.) Help.Adveritising.amazon.com. https://advertising.amazon.com/help?entityId=ENTITY2358XJVOPHN6

8 Google Ads Help. (n.d.) Quality Score: Definition. Google Ads. https://support.google.com/google-ads/answer/140351

9 Martelle, Craig. (March 26, 2018) Become a Successful Indie Author: Work Toward Your Writing Dream. Page 22.

Made in United States
North Haven, CT
30 May 2023